MOMENTS
of the Day

"In today's frenetic world, keeping the Lord's commandment to 'pray without ceasing' has never been more challenging. Collins shows us how we can meet this challenge in an elegant and practical introduction to the Apostleship of Prayer. *Three Moments of the Day* is nourishment for the soul, a welcome companion on the journey of faith."

Rev. Matt Malone, S.J.
President and Editor-in-Chief
America

"Fr. Chris Collins, S.J., has written a dynamic and entertaining invitation to the Church: let Jesus love us and heal us at the depth of our wounds. Collins carries this message of healing to us in joy and with a spiritual energy that is lodged in his mastery of the spiritual tradition of Catholicism. Here, in this accessible source, we can encounter the fire of the Sacred Heart, a fire of love searching for us all."

Deacon James Keating
Director of Theological Formation
Institute for Priestly Formation
Creighton University

"Fr. Collins has written an engaging book that shows us how to incorporate classic practices of prayer into active lives today. This simple yet profound program of three moments a day will bless all who undertake it. In this book, a rich spiritual content is conveyed in heartfelt and accessible language."

Timothy M. Gallagher, O.M.V.
Author of *The Discernment of Spirits*

"In *Three Moments of the Day*, Fr. Collins shines Ignatian light upon praying throughout the day to the Sacred Heart of Jesus. His practical, warm, and humorous narrative draws the reader along from one profound insight to the next as we enjoy his straightforward directions for opening our hearts more fully to Our Lord. This book will touch your heart. Begin reading it today, and try to live it always."

Ellen Mary Raster
St. Mary's Visitation Parish
Milwaukee, WI

Praying with the Heart of Jesus

MOMENTS
of the Day

Christopher S. Collins, S.J.

ave maria press AmP notre dame, indiana

© 2014 by Wisconsin Province of the Society of Jesuits

Founded in 1865, Ave Maria Press is a ministry of the United States Province of Holy Cross.

www.avemariapress.com

Paperback: ISBN-13 978-1-59471-464-1

E-book: ISBN-13 978-1-59471-465-8

Cover image © Corbis.

Cover and text design by David Scholtes.

Printed and bound in the United States of America.

Library of Congress Cataloging-in-Publication Data
Collins, Christopher S., 1971-
 Three moments of the day : praying with the heart of Jesus / Christopher S. Collins, S.J.
    pages cm
 Includes bibliographical references.
 ISBN 978-1-59471-464-1 (pbk.) -- ISBN 978-1-59471-465-8 (ebook)
 1. Prayer--Catholic Church. I. Title.
 BV210.3.C645 2014
 248.3'2--dc23

                    2014012305

Nothing is more practical than

finding God, than

falling in Love in a quite absolute, final way.

What you are in love with,

what seizes your imagination, will affect everything.

It will decide

what will get you out of bed in the morning,

what you do with your evenings,

how you spend your weekends,

what you read, whom you know,

what breaks your heart,

and what amazes you with joy and gratitude.

Fall in Love, stay in love,

and it will decide everything.

       —Pedro Arrupe, S.J., *Finding God in All Things*

Contents

• • •

Foreword

...

According to Dr. Victor Frankl, a psychiatrist who survived the Nazi concentration camps, the most basic human need is for meaning. Once a person's physical requirements are met, every human being needs to have a sense of purpose, a reason for living.

This deep sense of purpose is just as needed today, in a world dominated by what Pope Francis has called "a throwaway culture," which rejects as worthless those who are not productive and successful. The idea that there is some life not worthy of life is disturbingly similar to Nazi ideology.

What happens when we get to the point where we are no longer productive or when we are not successful as the world defines "success"? We are likely to ask these questions: "Why? Why am I here? What's the point?" In fact, at one time or another everyone faces these questions; each of us yearns to know the meaning or purpose of our own particular existence.

If you are wondering about these things, I have an important message for you: productive and successful or not, each one of us is beloved and important to God. As Pope Francis said in his homily for Divine Mercy Sunday in 2013: "For God, we are not numbers, we are important, indeed we are the most important thing to him; even if we are sinners, we are what is closest to his heart."

The Heart of Jesus is close to us. In the Eucharist, our hearts are united to his. This was made possible because the Son of God emptied himself and became flesh in order to give himself for the life of the world. His heart was pierced on the cross and always remains open to us.

When we know and receive God's love, our natural response is to want to return that love. Such a great, deep, and unfailing love, to quote Pope Francis again, invites a great and deep response. When we know that God has given all, our natural desire is to give all in return. But, practically speaking, how can we do that? Is it possible in our busy, flawed lives to give ourselves fully to God? Can we do it even for a day?

The answer is yes.

Think about the Eucharist. When we participate in the celebration of the Holy Sacrifice of the Mass, we unite ourselves to Jesus' perfect offering. He gives himself wholly to us and we give ourselves wholly to him. We go forth from Mass to live that offering in our daily lives.

The Apostleship of Prayer provides a way in which everyone can live faith in daily life, even if one is unable to attend Mass every day. In this book, Fr. Christopher Collins, S.J., explores the simple and profound spirituality of the Apostleship of Prayer. He describes the three moments of prayer that allow us to walk closely with God. Each of the three moments are centered on offering, just as the Eucharist is centered on offering.

We begin each day by accepting that day as a gift from God and offering it back to him. Then we try to live our day conscious of the offering that we have made, reminding ourselves from time to time to offer up the moments of the day—the prayers, works, joys, and sufferings. And, at the end of the day, we look back on the offering we've made both with gratitude for the role we have played in the ongoing salvation of the world and with sorrow for those things in the day we offered which were really not worthy of God.

These are the three moments of the day that make life worthwhile. They give us a meaning and purpose beyond anything else because by means of them we are fulfilling our destiny. Through them we love God, and we show that love by loving our neighbor. Every precious moment of time has eternal significance, either contributing to the salvation of our neighbor or not. Every moment, no matter how small, routine, or seemingly insignificant, has great significance in God's eyes when it is joined to the perfect offering of Jesus. Those now-significant moments of our lives actually play a role in the salvation of souls.

This book illustrates how we can take advantage of opportunities to do great good in little and large ways! The key, says Fr. Collins, is to offer our days, every day, one by one. Within each day, we learn to give and to live each moment as an act of love for God. Then at the end of each day, we review the day we offered, gratefully preparing to give ourselves again in the morning. In this way you and I will become the saints God has created us to be.

James Kubicki, S.J.
National Director of the Apostleship of Prayer

Stumbling into the
Three Moments

. . .

The favors of the Lord are not exhausted,

his mercies are not spent;

They are renewed each morning,

so great is his faithfulness.

—Lamentations 3:22–23

I had never paid attention to images of the Heart of Jesus before I joined the Society of Jesus (Jesuits). Even though I grew up in a solid Catholic family and went to Catholic schools all my life, the Sacred Heart never penetrated my dense little consciousness. But soon after I joined the Jesuits at the age of twenty-three, I read a book by Fr. Pedro Arrupe, an earlier superior general who played a major role in reforming and updating the Jesuit Order after the Second Vatican Council.

Fr. Arrupe helped our order to get in sync with the times. But Fr. Arrupe was also critical of the times, believing that Catholics as a whole and Jesuits in particular had lost touch with what might be called a *devotional imagination*. He reminded us that devotion to the Heart of Christ—that is, devotion to the love God shows us in the flesh of his Son whose loving Heart was pierced on the Cross—should remain the center of our lives. It is Christ's Heart that speaks of God's will for us. God's love, demonstrated in the flesh by Jesus, is the source of our hope. Arrupe even went so far as to say that the renewal of the devotion to the Sacred Heart would be a sign of the renewal of the Society of Jesus. As a brand-new Jesuit, I took note of this, though honestly I didn't really know what it meant and what it would soon come to mean in my own life.

Only a few months later, in bleak midwinter, I was sent by my novice master to Pine Ridge, South Dakota. This was not a vacation. I had accepted a mission to teach students at Red Cloud Indian School, which is a work of our mission on the reservation there. I was also commissioned to drive the school bus in the afternoons and do odd jobs around the place.

Now, any teacher will tell you that coming to a school in the middle of the year is difficult under the best of circumstances. However, I had taught high school for two years, and so I thought I would probably be successful in the classroom here. I was mistaken.

Because of the cultural and religious differences between the Native American students and their mostly white teachers, many students did not trust their teachers. This was especially true of me, the newcomer. Every day after I had finished teaching and driving the afternoon bus, I would come back to the community chapel and just sit there. I thought I was praying, but in reality I was just talking to myself about my woes.

I was being beaten in the classroom day in and day out. What I eagerly wanted to give them, these Lakota teenagers did not want. They had grown up on the reservation with a suspicion of white people in general and of priests and religious in particular. Many associated Christianity with the forces of colonialism that had oppressed them and left them bereft of their culture and their way of life. This made sense. But it also put up barriers. The students and I were both carrying a lot of historical baggage.

At first I was angry with the kids: *What's their problem? How can they be so disrespectful and ungrateful?* Then I would be angry with their parents for not raising them right. Soon, however, I turned that angry judging of others onto myself. I had much to accuse myself of. The problem wasn't so much with the students but with the teacher. *If you knew what you were doing in there*, I said to myself, *you would be able to handle the classroom. You thought you were a successful teacher already, but it's clear now that you're a fraud. If you weren't so lazy and ill prepared, you might be able to come up with a lesson plan that would work!*

Encountering the Sacred Heart

Obviously, my afternoons in the chapel judging the kids and their parents and then berating myself made for some pretty messy prayer times. But then one day as I sat in the chapel, I noticed a statue outside the door to the hallway, just beyond the tabernacle. For some reason this little painted plaster image drew my attention.

It was my first personal encounter with the Sacred Heart. Jesus was standing there with his Heart opened up, vulnerable, on the outside of his body. The Heart was pierced and bloody, and the plaster itself was dinged up quite a bit. I noticed his hands, too; one pointed to his heart, the other beckoned to me. There he stood, looking at me with such intense love; it was as if he was speaking directly to me, saying, "This is the way I live. This is the way I love. Truly, this is the only way to love. You can do it. You must do it. There is no other way."

As I looked at the statue, what drew me in was the pierced Heart. That's how my heart felt. Mine was getting pierced in smaller ways than Jesus' Heart but in very real ways nonetheless. I had given myself to this religious vocation. And now I wanted to share what had been happening in my heart with kids who I knew desperately needed to hear some good news, and yet they wanted none of it. Not only was I proving to be a lame teacher but also that perhaps my whole vocation was for nothing. As they rejected me every day, my students were in a small but real way piercing my heart. I could see Jesus' Heart had been pierced long before mine, but maybe his Heart was continuing to be pierced right along with mine. I suddenly saw that I was not alone.

More important, I began to situate this whole context into a larger framework. The piercings my students had undergone in their own lives were far greater than anything I was feeling. I started to see all of this—my own suffering, the suffering of those around me, and the suffering found in the whole of human history—as marked by wounds of various degrees and kinds. And now I was beginning to see all of it in light of the pierced Heart of Christ.

But that Heart was more than just pierced. I also saw the fire emerging out of it. Even though the piercings are real, continuous wounds, they do not destroy his Heart. He could take the piercings, all the way to death, even, and still live. And it wasn't a matter of taking the pain in some heroic, stoic, tough-guy way. I could see in a new way that Jesus had a way of transforming these sufferings into fire, into life, and into love. The piercings and the fire of that Heart had started to sink into my imagination, and I began to see with the eyes of my own heart how the piercings and the fire go together. They are not contradictory. In fact, the power and brightness of the fire is made possible only by the piercings.

If I try to avoid piercing, I might be able to for a while, but then the fire will go out. I can build up barriers around my heart to make sure I don't get disappointed or hurt. I can become cynical and bitter and not get my hopes up to avoid the hurt of disappointment. I can numb my heart as our culture encourages us through entertainment, distraction, pornography, drug and alcohol abuse, workaholism—you name it. I can try any number of ways to numb or protect my heart, to build a barrier around it, and in every case the fire will go out. What I'd have on my hands then would be a hardened and lifeless heart, not good for much at all. I might be walking around, but I'd be dead inside.

Once I began to see the Sacred Heart in this way, it became clear to me that this was all I needed. I saw, and still see, that this is all there is. This is the whole of reality. The point of our lives is love. There is no love without piercings along the way, but the piercings will not do us in. I will be wounded along the way living this life, living this vocation, but I can remain on fire. There is a fire that will not be quenched if I keep my heart open, if I resist the temptations to shut down, to defend, and to hide. This is Jesus. His whole mission has always been to open up the Heart of God to the world and not flinch in doing so.

I would later come across a U2 song that spoke to this reality. In "When I Look at the World," Bono sings in a kind of dialogue with Jesus, or maybe better, a wondering soliloquy directed at Jesus. He sings of imagining the world through Jesus' eyes.

> People find all kinds of things that bring them to
> their knees. . . .

> So I try to be like you, try to feel it like you do,
>   but without you it's no use. . . .
>
> Can't wait . . . to see what you see when I look at
>   the world.[1]

The Christian imagination and Christian prayer in daily life must start, I believe, with this sense of wonder at Jesus—who he is and how he lives and loves. What has God done, letting go of his power, of his transcendence to become small and vulnerable, first as a baby in the womb of a young woman? What has he done, to be born into a stable and laid in a manger that animals eat out of, and then to end his life on earth in humiliation and defeat on a cross, executed between two common criminals? What has God done? This isn't how God is supposed to act!

And if this is God, then who am I? What does it mean to live authentically? As a follower of Jesus, how am I following his example of love? By keeping my gaze on Jesus, I start to see my own daily interactions with people a bit differently. To do this, I need to pray in a way that will keep me in constant dialogue, prayerfully mindful of seeing the events of my life through the lens of the Heart of Jesus.

Can I live like that? Can I love like that? Pausing a few times during the day to ask those questions and to cultivate a vision based on the Heart of Jesus, is the goal.

Finding Our True Selves in the Sacred Heart

At a conference dedicated to the history and theology of devotion to the Sacred Heart in 1981, then Cardinal Joseph Ratzinger presented a paper on the foundations of the devotion to the

Heart of Jesus.[2] The future pope observed that devotion to the Sacred Heart is not simply one devotion among many. Rather, devotion to the Sacred Heart is *the* Christian devotion. The Sacred Heart of Jesus reveals the whole Christian mystery. In the words of Pope Benedict XVI: "The Christian God has a heart of flesh."

When I look at the image of the Sacred Heart, I see at once the image of God who has assumed a heart of flesh (Incarnation) that is wounded and bloodied (paschal mystery) and at the same time aflame with an unquenchable fire of love (Resurrection). And if this Heart signifies who Christ is, then it also points to who I am called to be. I can find my true self in living according to this vision.

My daily prayer, then, should lead me to live in this way: opened to the world, vulnerable, and simultaneously pierced and burning with love. If I can do this, I need never lose hope, for I will have accomplished God's ultimate vision, the purpose for which I was created.

So, how can I pray in such a way that disposes me to become more and more like this—united to the Heart of Christ?

Rediscover the Daily Prayer of the Heart

Over time, some Jesuit friends and I adopted a method of prayer that we later discovered had been established long before we took up the practice. This approach involves offering my heart and my life to God at three separate "moments" of each day.

At the beginning of the day, I say to Jesus, "I want to live this day, and all that's in it, not in isolation but with you. I want to offer what's in my heart to what's in your Heart."

At the end of the day, I take another moment to look back and see how it's gone. This prayer, or Examen, is based on one of the ways of praying taught by St. Ignatius of Loyola in his Spiritual Exercises. This is a simple act of using memory to pay attention to what actually happened in the day. Little by little, I developed a habit of speaking to Jesus about all that is ordinary in my life. As I continued this daily practice of engaging in brief exchanges every morning and evening, it began to change how I looked at the world.

The third "moment" covers the spiritual reality of the whole day. We might think of this moment as a continuation of the celebration of the Eucharist, the source and summit of our lives. Whether or not we attended Mass on a particular day, the ordinariness of everyday life is best understood in light of this "moment" of prayer in which the whole Church engages all over the world, every day. Although you and I cannot be physically present at every moment and in every place this prayer is being offered, we are a part of this mystery. What goes on in the Eucharist gives me a framework for understanding and making choices in daily life that will lead me out of isolation and into relationship, into dialogue, and into friendship with God.

This "three moments" approach to prayer is not about "punching the clock" with God; we are not God's employees. We are his children. And so, we offer our lives to God, day by day, in the same way that Jesus offered his life and days to the Father. This is a way of praying and seeing the world that starts to make our daily lives much more intimate, as places of genuine encounter with God. Our day-to-day living, seen from within this way of praying, becomes a matter of one heart being offered to another. What sparked this discovery for me was the "discovery" of what I came to realize was called the Sacred Heart of Jesus.

In the chapters that follow, we will examine each of these moments in turn, so that you can begin to integrate them in your own life. For easy reference, you will find "The Three Moments: A Concise Guide" on page 137 to help you cultivate these daily prayer habits.

As you start praying like this, little by little, you will get in the habit of speaking to Jesus about all that is ordinary in your life. Then you'll begin to realize that by speaking about it to him, things are starting to change—or you are changing. Everything is changing. Things might not have gotten fixed the way you asked or expected, but they did get fixed. These brief exchanges of speaking and listening during the day will change the landscape of your life. This prayer practice can change how you see the world.

An Invitation

Most of us feel far from God at times. Oftentimes, we attribute this distance to our busyness or our self-sufficiency; we are too busy to pray or don't feel we need God. Other times, it is guilt or shame that separates us, our fear of what God thinks of us, or our presumption that God has better things to do than to get wrapped up in the little things of our lives.

At times we may feel as if there is a great and widening chasm between God and us and that the prospect of trying to cross that gap is overwhelming. As we read in *Gaudium et spes*, "Through Christ and in Christ, the riddles of sorrow and death grow meaningful. Apart from His Gospel, they overwhelm us."[3]

So then, how can we span the great gulf between God and ourselves? Can we pray ourselves across it? That sounds like a very tough job, requiring lots of discipline and incredible focus. Don't be afraid. Start by making an offering, and then watch what happens.

Daily Offering Prayer of St. Thérèse of Lisieux Member of the Apostleship of Prayer

Oh my God! I offer You all my actions of this day for the intentions and for the glory of the Sacred Heart of Jesus. I desire to sanctify every beat of my heart, my every thought, my simplest works, by uniting them to His infinite merits; and I wish to make reparation for my sins by casting them in the furnace of His merciful love.

Oh my God! I ask of You for myself and for those dear to me the grace to fulfill perfectly Your holy will, to accept for love of You the joys and sorrows of this passing life, so that we may one day be united together in heaven for all eternity. Amen.

Questions and Reflections

1. At what moments do you feel far from God?

2. Do you have any ideas why?

3. How do you talk to yourself in ways that block you from God?

4. Recall and savor a genuine heart-to-heart conversation with God.

5. What do you think Jesus would say to you now from his Heart?

6. What does your heart long to tell Jesus at this moment? Tell him.

PART I

The Morning Offering

• • •

A Morning Offering

Jesus,

I offer you my day and all that is in it—all the prayers, works, joys, and sufferings I might experience today—in union with your own Heart that is loved by the Father and opened up to the world, even if it gets pierced. I offer you every moment of the day in union also with the intentions of the Holy Father, all the bishops around the world, and all other apostles of prayer, as well as with all those who are suffering today, for the salvation of the world. Amen.

The Morning Offering

. . .

Though he was in the form of God, did not regard equality with God something to be grasped. Rather, he emptied himself, taking the form of a slave, coming in human likeness; and found human in appearance, he humbled himself, becoming obedient to death, even death on a cross.

—Philippians 2:6–8

If we want to get closer to God, we must speak with him frequently in prayer. Okay, fine. But how exactly do we do that? What if we don't feel up to the task?

Actually, we aren't up to that task. Admitting that fact is a good place to start. No one of us is worthy, no one deserves an audience with the holy, all-powerful Creator of the universe. And yet, over and over again God reaches out to us. St. Paul wrote that, when we don't have the right words to pray, the Spirit prays within us (see Rom 8:26–27). St. Irenaeus said that the Word of God was "made flesh" so that we might unite ourselves with immortality.[4]

> This is the reason why the Word of God was made flesh . . . so that we might enter into communion with the Word of God, and by receiving adoption might become sons of God. Indeed we should not be able to share in immortality without a close union with the Immortal.[5]

Something new happened in human history after God became a person. When the Father sent the Son to take on human flesh, God made himself part of our human story. Now, it's for us in daily prayer, throughout the three moments of each day, to recognize how we are part of God's story.

What I suggest in this chapter is a way of praying that is not a big secret. It doesn't require flawless discipline, specialized technique, or prerequisite holiness. It's a way of praying at the beginning of the day that simply offers to God everything that makes up our ordinary lives. He's already become a part of the human story. The Morning Offering prayer is a way for us to consciously insert our ordinary day into God's hands and make it a part of God's story.

Getting Started

Many Catholics who grew up in previous generations have told me that one of the main prayers they learned as children, after the Our Father and the Hail Mary, was the Morning Offering of the Apostleship of Prayer. One man I know, a retired university administrator, recently told me that he started posting the Morning Offering on his bathroom window in the 1940s, as a student at a Jesuit school, and has been praying it every morning since. I think there are many such prayers scrawled on slips of paper and stuck onto windows and mirrors and nooks and crannies in the homes of older Catholics. I think it would be a great help to lots of younger people to take up that same practice.

I grew up without knowing about this practice. Once in a while, if I was complaining about something, my mom might annoy me by saying, "Offer it up." That was as close as I came to the Morning Offering—or the Apostleship of Prayer that promotes this way of praying—until I joined the Jesuits. Since I've started doing it, though, it's made a great difference in my life. It helps dispose me to make everything I do each day an expression of prayer. It helps me align my will with God's. It syncs my heart with the Heart of Christ, helping me to see others as he sees them and to live among others motivated by God's love. (Maybe Mom knew what she was talking about!)

I'm not saying the Morning Offering is a spiritual panacea. It doesn't make everything work out perfectly in my daily life. I get distracted. I forget about the offering I made at the beginning of the day as things start to get complicated. But at least I began my day right. I made the offering today. And again another day. And day by day, little by little, that practice has come to shape my imagination and the way I begin to see my life, the lives of other people, and the world around me. At the very least, the Morning Offering is a good starting point that gives me purpose and direction even if I lose it along the way in my busy day.

There are dozens of offering prayers out there. Here's the version I pray:

> O Jesus, through the Immaculate Heart of Mary,
> I offer you my prayers, works, joys, and sufferings
> of this day
> in union with the Holy Sacrifice of the Mass
> throughout the world.
> I offer them for all the intentions of your Sacred
> Heart:
> the salvation of souls, reparation for sin, and the
> reunion of all Christians.
> I offer them for the intentions of our bishops and
> of all apostles of prayer,

and in particular for those recommended by our
Holy Father this month.
Amen.

Notice that the "reach" of this Morning Offering is not a laundry list of petitions; rather, after addressing Jesus directly and invoking the friendship of his mother, the prayer goes right to its main thrust: "*I* offer *you* . . ." Speaking to Jesus, I am offering him my day—all of it—the good, the bad, and the ugly. What can seem like a whole litany of duties that I have to take care of on my own now becomes a joint effort. Not just the spiritual, "churchy" things that I do but all of it—the prayers *and* the works, the joys *and* the sufferings—becomes part of one coherent expression of who I am.

Jesus wants to be a part of it all. He wants to live the *whole day* with me, not just what I think he ought to be interested in or approving of. My whole day then has the potential to become something undertaken, in dialogue, in friendship with the Lord who has already joined his life to mine. To make this joint effort truly personal, it's essential to speak from the heart and let Jesus unite his Heart to mine in all that I do.

A Family Offering

I encountered a variation on the Morning Offering a couple of years ago when I found out that my sister had initiated an evening ritual in her house with her two kids. They called it "prayers, works, joys, and sufferings." I think they learned it from another family in their parish. My sister and her kids aren't super religious, but this is something that they all started to appreciate. (Of course, the kids bellyached about it at first, but after a while they'd complain if they missed it one night.)

Toward the end of dinner, everyone would go around the table and say what the prayers and works were of the day—who they wanted to pray for and something they worked hard on, usually at school. Then they'd cover the joys and the sufferings too. It took only a few minutes, but it was obviously a good exercise for them all, if for nothing else, just to remember what went on in the day. This breaks the rut. But also, they were sharing their lives together and, maybe even somewhat unconsciously, sharing it with God. I don't think they even considered themselves to be praying, but they were giving an opening to the Lord, letting him in on the regular stuff of their lives, precisely by sharing it in the context of their evening meal. My sister also liked it because she could get little insights into what was going on in her kids' lives. She learned things that she might not have been aware of and thereby knew where to pay extra attention in caring for them in the near future.

Speaking these moments of a day out loud (and together) is a great foundation for cultivating a spirituality of the Morning Offering and evening review (Examen) that we will discuss later. It disposes us to being able to recognize God in daily life. St. Thérèse of Lisieux, who was herself a card-carrying member of the Apostleship of Prayer, called this "the Little Way"—finding union with God in the little things. She was able to do that, in part, because she disposed herself to it every morning when she made her offering.

Listening, Speaking, and Looking

In his inaugural offerings on Twitter, Pope Benedict was forced to be brief and to the point—140 characters or less, right? Someone asked him how to live the Year of Faith well. He responded, "By *speaking* with Jesus in prayer, *listening* to what he tells you in the Gospel, and *looking* for him in those in need." That nails it, don't you think?

The same advice may be applied to how the Lord wants us to spend each day. We start by speaking with Jesus about our hopes and fears, and listening to him speak to our hearts as we enter the day. Then, when we are out in the world, we are better able to see him, especially in the vulnerable. The Morning Offering orients us to live this way. In it, we make a simple act of faith, hope, and love. The brief prayer gets the ball rolling in the right direction. If we make this offering in the very first moment we wake up in the morning, it orients our imagination and desires for the rest of the day, with all it holds, whether it seems pertinent to our faith or not. We are prepared to seek God in all things.

Why Make This Offering in the Morning?

Why is it important to make a daily offering in the morning, perhaps even before getting out of bed? The instant we awaken, each moment is full of potential: to meet Christ and to be strengthened by his friendship or to wander away from Christ and get stuck in isolation. Even though this day may seem like just another day, each one blurring into the next, there's really a lot riding on *today*. Because of this potential for closeness with God, I want to open up the eyes and ears of my heart as soon as possible each day, so that I might see and hear where God is present and communicating love to me and to others in the world.

When I say to Christ, "I offer you all my prayers, works, joys, and sufferings," I'm reminding myself that today will bring some good and some bad. There will be some moments I will want to receive in gratitude. I will want to be able to savor them when they come. There will also be pitfalls: sad news in the paper over breakfast, getting out there in morning traffic, the tedious meeting at 10:00 a.m., or the snarky comment of a coworker, spouse, or child—any number of things in this day might bring me down.

Once we've made a Morning Offering, we can look at each day's schedule from that perspective with both potential graces and potential pitfalls. We can ask the Lord to be with us in a special way in that challenging meeting, or when we encounter the one person that always seems to hit a nerve or put us on the defensive. There will be lots of surprises today as well, but why not gear up in the presence of Jesus for those moments that we *know* will be tough?

The Morning Offering—that simple, daily act of faith, hope, and love—also demands the use of some *reason* when considering our daily living. We can be smart about knowing where the graces and the pitfalls are based on past experience. The Morning Offering with the specifics of the day in mind can be an occasion to have a brief chat with Jesus about things ahead: "Lord, I know that conversation with that person is going to be tough today. I get taken down every time I speak with her. Just be with me in it. Help me to be more confident and peaceful in the encounter. Help me avoid saying anything sharp or nasty in the midst of it! If some hostility comes my way, help me to take it, in love, as you do. Help me to take those little piercings of my heart, united to your heart."

Letting Jesus in ahead of time this way, *before* the day gets tough, is a great thing to do if we remember to do it. Of course, if you're like me, you don't usually think of asking his help with a tough situation until it's already a big mess. But a habit of praying the Morning Offering helps us at least to sensitize our hearts and to be a bit quicker to invite Jesus in where we most need him.

One difficulty we often have in prayer is that we tend to think prayer should be clean and holy—disciplined and controlled. But sometimes prayers that are nice and neat feel cut off from the mess that is our real lives. The spirituality of the Morning Offering recognizes that Jesus wants to redeem every bit of our lives, not just the "holy" parts we present to him.

In his play *Heauton Timorumenos*, the Roman poet Terence, who predated Jesus by a century or two, observed, "Because I am human, nothing human is foreign to me." Later, Christian writers recognized and expanded upon this humanist sentiment in light of the Incarnation, God assuming human life. Christian humanism suggests that God has already inserted himself into every part of the human story in the person of Jesus. It's now up to us to continue to cooperate and invite him into the whole of our story, so that he might redeem it.

An Invitation

To begin each day asking for grace to live with the Heart of Christ opens a world of possibility to us. The Morning Offering allows us to entrust our work as well as every moment of our lives into the hands of the Lord. He wants us to live in his love, to live the full, thriving, holy, and joyful life we were created to live. He alone can help us do that, as we live united to the Heart of Jesus. His Heart has received the fullness of the Father's love, and thus Jesus is confident enough to be opened up to the world, a Heart pierced, bloodied, and eternally on fire. And yet, it is a Heart that is never "done in."

That can be my heart and your heart, too. We can participate in the fire of God's love by offering to Jesus all the stuff of our days—what is good and what is tough as well. We give ourselves to him in love because he first gave himself to us. By doing so, we let Jesus take over our hearts little by little so that we can become what God created us to be: his children, living in the image of his Son, and our hearts one with his Heart.

A Morning Offering

O Jesus, through the Immaculate Heart of Mary,
I offer you my prayers, works, joys, and sufferings of
    this day
in union with the Holy Sacrifice of the Mass throughout
    the world.
I offer them for all the intentions of your Sacred Heart:
the salvation of souls, reparation for sin, and the reunion
    of all Christians.
I offer them for the intentions of our bishops and of all
    apostles of prayer,
and in particular for those recommended by our Holy
    Father this month.
Amen.

Questions and Reflections

1. How might you live differently if you offered your day to God?

2. What is frightening about making an offering to God of every bit of your day?

3. Use a day planner or calendar for your Morning Offering. This gives some particulars to offer to the Lord.

4. Do you want to offer your day for a particular person or intention? Make a note of it. Call the person or intention to mind at the beginning of the day and then remember him or her at the end of the day.

For the Salvation of the World

• • •

Now I rejoice in my sufferings for your sake, and in my flesh I am filling up what is lacking in the afflictions of Christ on behalf of his body, which is the church.

—Colossians 1:24

"To find God in all things" is perhaps the aspect of Ignatian spirituality best known today. And yet, as far as we know, St. Ignatius never actually used that particular phrase. Rather, he urged his fellow Jesuits to "*seek* God in all things."

Seeking God in all things is an ongoing practice. It requires desire. It requires attentiveness. But because God's constant desire is to show himself to us, the presumption is that God can indeed be found if we do seek. God can be encountered not only in spiritual, religious, and "churchy" experiences but also in all kinds of other ways, including the most mundane and when things are kind of a mess. We can find God whenever we seek him, in our successes, brokenness, and failures. Indeed, perhaps God can especially be found in our failures. God became one of us in order to redeem and bring healing to every part of our brokenness.

A Great Debate

In the first centuries of Church history, the Church fathers debated the nature of Christ, whether or not Jesus was really human. Curiously, among early Christians, the question wasn't whether Jesus was divine but rather whether he was really human as are the rest of us. Few in the early Christian communities doubted whether Jesus could save as God saves. The question was, what was he saving?

One argument went like this: As Christians, we believe the risen Jesus is the Christ. We know we are being saved by him. But if Jesus is not fully human, like us, then the salvation that we experience by being in communion with him does not get to the core of what we need from him, from God. God must have taken on every bit of the human condition if his love and mercy, his grace, and his salvation are going to be able to touch the *whole* of our humanity. St. Irenaeus put it more succinctly: "What has not been assumed [by God] cannot be redeemed."

What does it mean to say that God "assumed" our humanity? It means that God himself *united* himself to all that is part of human nature except for sin, which in fact is not really a part of our true human nature anyway. In the Incarnation and again at the Cross, Jesus united himself to us who are very unlike God so that we might be redeemed—every part of us. And so, no matter where we seek God in our human condition, we can find him. And where our condition is wounded by sin and disorder, we can find him there, too, trying to draw us back to himself.

Why bother with all this theology? What difference does it make in our praying relationship with God that God has become human? Understanding the truth about who Jesus is, and what he has done for us since God assumed humanity, has everything to do with how we can and must relate to God. That God became human has everything to do with the character of our prayer. Because of this reality, every aspect of our lives, if we offer it to the Lord, becomes a place of great holiness and light—even what had seemed dark and far removed from God.

It is especially true that when things fall apart, we turn to God—and rightly so! When was the last time you asked someone to pray for you? I'll bet things were pretty bad when it happened. When things are broken and it looks as if there is no way we can put it back together, it sets off a kind of chain reaction of the heart. Suddenly, we are open and vulnerable, willing to turn to others to ask for prayers. It might be for the loved one with cancer, the son or daughter going off the rails, or the friend who lost a job or was injured in a car accident. And yet, how much more should we turn to the Lord and express our needs directly to him when we need him most?

Sometimes, if we are not regular prayers, we may feel as if we are being hypocritical to do this. God does not think of it as we do, though. What is important to God (and to us) is that our hearts are opening and we are realizing that we are not in control. We need others. We need God. We need to be in relationship. And if painful moments of separation expose this need to us, then so be it. It's for our good. We have already been saved but also not yet saved, as Catholic theologians like to say, "already" and "not yet." Christ is the savior, but *the way* he saves mysteriously relies upon people like us and how we live, how we *offer* our daily lives.

That's why our daily offering prayer is so essential. It's our way of reminding ourselves that this day means a lot. The salvation of the world quite literally depends upon it! So whether I'm at my desk crunching numbers, at home changing diapers, or lying in a hospital bed, I am potentially helping Christ redeem the world by uniting my heart to his. We make an offering of the day with an eye toward the places of our lives, our church, and our world where things are broken and don't seem to be able to be put back together.

An Offering That Makes a Difference

In the Morning Offering, we give Jesus our *sufferings* as well as our *joys*. Let's consider the way our sufferings work in the big picture. When we are suffering, sometimes we feel alone in our pain; this sense of isolation can seem so pointless. And yet, we aren't really alone. Praying the Morning Offering dispels such lies.

Though we might forget later in the day, at least during our Morning Offering we know that all that happens today in our lives, in our own little corner of the world, is not happening in isolation. It is happening in union with the Heart of Christ. What is happening today in my life is in fact a *part of Jesus's mission to redeem the world* and all human history. And by the way, he has already won the victory in the struggle in which we are still engaged!

In his letter to the Colossians, St. Paul acknowledged this when he wrote that his own sufferings and the sufferings of the people in Colossus can be fruitful because they are "filling up what is lacking in the afflictions of Christ" (Col 1:24). So our sufferings can also make up for what is *lacking* in the sufferings of Christ. The first time I heard that, I had to go look it up to make sure that was actually in the Bible. I didn't understand it. What could be *lacking* in the sufferings of Christ? How could our sufferings be necessary to help complete or fulfill the mission of Christ?

Slowly it began to make sense to me. Christ has indeed won the victory by his suffering and dying on the Cross and his subsequent resurrection, but the battle isn't over yet. Somehow in the mystery of God, we, the mystical Body of Christ, the Church, can and must take part in the mission of Christ if we hope for the salvation of the world. In fact, at Mass we pray for this, in the third Eucharistic Prayer: "May this sacrifice of our reconciliation we pray, O Lord, *advance the peace and salvation of all the world.*"

The sufferings we go through on a daily basis—when we turn them into expressions of love and unite them to the Heart of Christ offered in daily Mass around the world—can and do have an effect on the salvation of the world. That's what we say when we pray at Mass. What if it's true?

Suffering Transformed by Love

What if it's really true that our sufferings strengthen our prayers and help in the salvation of others? That seems like a game changer to me. First, we no longer need to feel we're alone in our tough times. Nor is our pain pointless. The wounds that we experience in our hearts find their place within the wounds of Christ's own Heart. And we know how that story ends—in triumph, in resurrection. So we know where our sufferings are headed if they are united to the Heart of Christ in simple, trusting love even if we don't know *how* God will make our sufferings pay off for the salvation of others.

But it's not only our own wounds that concern us, though those might be the ones that get us going in heartfelt prayer at the beginning. Once we start praying to live our days united to the Heart of Christ, pretty soon we start to see with his eyes a bit more. We start to feel with his Heart. We start to look around and see others who are wounded. We see those who are lost, who are hungry—physically, emotionally, and spiritually. We see those who are in need of receiving love, and our hearts are moved with pity for the vulnerable in the habit of the Heart of the One who is "moved with pity" for us (Mk 6:34).

Presenting Our Intentions to the Heart of Christ

In the course of the Morning Offering, we consciously unite our days and all that is in them *for* particular intentions.

First, we unite our intentions to those of the Church. We pray first for the intentions of the Heart of Jesus and then for the whole Church, for all the other people who are praying this same prayer daily, and for the intentions of the bishops and especially for those of the pope, who has a universal vision of what is needed.

Then we offer our day, and all that is in it, for the salvation of souls. Offering our days with intentionality has an effect that extends well beyond us. And yet, it is transformative to us as well, to how we view the world around us. When people like us start to unite our lives and our hearts in one another and in the Heart of Christ, things will change.

The primary purpose of the Apostleship of Prayer, it must be remembered, is ultimately the *salvation of all souls*. That is our hope. And we want to remember and help those who need the most help getting to God. With our small but concrete acts of love, we help those who are farthest from God by creating a pathway of love, a bridge back to God.

In our offerings, we offer our days in *reparation for our own sins* and for those of others. We acknowledge concrete places where, in words or actions, we have already created a distance or separation from God; we make a little act of repairing that bridge back home. We recognize the harm that has been done and seek to restore the relationship where it has been broken.

Through prayer, all these things are drawn into the Heart of Jesus, into the friendship that is God—the love between the Father, Son, and Holy Spirit. Wherever there is separation from this love, Jesus sees and is wounded by it and desires its healing. Those who pray united to his Heart start to see things this way too.

Of course, there will be times when, no matter how frequently we offer a particular intention, and no matter what we do, we are unable to "bridge the gap." Even in these cases, we can offer up our own difficulties and sufferings as an expression of love in solidarity with those who feel far off, so that all *those* divides might be healed.

We pray for the unity of all Christians. In each Morning Offering we unite our intentions with those of Christ, who prayed "that they may all be one, as you, Father, are in me and I in you, that they also may be in us, that the world may believe that you sent me" (Jn 17:20–21). The separation of Christians from one another is a great scandal, for it is the exact opposite of what Jesus came to bring—unity. The Christian community is not what it should be because of that separation; as followers of Jesus, we must do what we can to restore that brokenness as well.

In our daily lives, each of us can name our brokenness, within ourselves and within our communities, and deliberately invite Jesus to be with us and with all those who are separated from us. We can "offer up" our daily trials and sufferings so that God might unite them with the sufferings of the Heart of Jesus and bring about the unity that the Lord intended for his Church.

In so doing, we become living signs of the love of God in the world. With each Morning Offering, we are helping those who are on their way to the final judgment, so that they might be drawn into the fullness of salvation in Christ; we are helping undo (repair) some of the mess that we and our fellow Christians have made by our own sins; and maybe somehow we are a part of the solution to bring all Christians back into union with one another around the world. When we unite our hearts daily to others and to the Heart of the Lord, we start to pray from within and take part in Jesus' own prayer to the Father that "they might all be one." And yet, we must begin by having the courage to recognize where things are broken, where there is hurt, and take seriously these piercings in our own hearts and in the Heart of Christ.

Solidarity in the Eucharist

With each Morning Offering, we commit to live this day in solidarity with Jesus who offers himself to the Church in the Eucharist. We commit ourselves to live in solidarity with the whole Church who receives that Eucharist:

> I offer [this day] for the intentions of our bishops
> and of all apostles of prayer, and in particular
> for those recommended by our Holy Father this
> month.

This is the vision: You and I are not alone in our joys and sufferings. We are with Jesus in all of it. He is with us. But it's not just a "me-and-Jesus thing" as we face the mess of this world. In the Morning Offering, we turn outward from ourselves and courageously face the world in union with the whole Church.

We unite ourselves to the intentions and desires of all the bishops who have their eyes open to the needs of the world. We unite our hearts with the millions of apostles of prayer throughout the world who are making this same Morning Offering this day. We are consoled that they have the same vision as we do for living ordinary lives with ups and downs similar to what we are experiencing.

And finally, we offer the day united to the monthly intentions of the Holy Father. Each month for more than 150 years—and communicated to the whole Church around the world by the Apostleship of Prayer—the pope asks us to pray with him in his special intentions.[6]

With the global vision he has by virtue of his office, the pope highlights certain human needs in various parts of the world and among diverse groups of people so that we can pray for them too. One month it could be people with mental disabilities; another, it could be people suffering famine in Africa or war in the Middle East. The pope may ask us to pray for those left out of social and economic structures in Latin America or those suffering the deprivation of religious liberty in China or Vietnam. He might ask prayers for young mothers in difficult pregnancies, for confidence and compassion for missionaries in Oceania, or for a renewed vision of spiritual reality and truth for young people in Europe or the United States enthralled by materialism.

The needs of the world are endless, but the Holy Father focuses our intentions so that together we can remember this or that group of people in any given month. And in this focusing of our intentions, we know that our daily offering is somehow mystically, but *really* helping people we will probably never meet in the flesh. And yet in this offering of my day for their needs, we come to know them and are drawn into friendship and solidarity with them by virtue of this simple Morning Offering. All of a sudden what seemed like just another drab, dreary day in St. Louis, Roanoke, or Fresno starts to take on depth and significance in the life of the universal Church, the Body of Christ.

Global Solidarity in the Mystical Body of Christ

This way of praying is all about getting specific and concrete—in our own lives and in the needs of the world, as well as in the particular love that Christ calls us all to experience. St. Ignatius always stressed that we do well to be *specific* in articulating what we desire from the Lord. We do this so that we might receive the graces he sends to us with greater intentionality and joy.

Joining in the particular monthly intentions of the pope each day, and then trying to live in solidarity with those people, is a way for the ordinary members of the Church throughout the world to do something extraordinary for people on the other side of the world. In this prayer, we unite our hearts to theirs in love and remember people with particular needs so different from our own, and yet somehow the same. These little acts of solidarity draw us closer together as one body in Christ.

What makes this prayer so powerful is that it touches upon what we share in common, the places of pain, suffering, and vulnerability that every person around the world experiences in various ways. Together we approach the pierced and enflamed Heart of Christ. These places of vulnerability, places in our hearts that at times seem to have grown dead and hopeless, become places of great hope and holiness, and places where we meet God—together.

Vulnerability at the Heart of Reality

A few years ago, I heard an episode of a program called *On Being* on National Public Radio. They profiled a French geophysicist named Xavier Le Pichon. He is one of the founders of the discipline that has come to be known as plate tectonics. He came to recognize that when the earth's plates move and crash into each other, great devastation occurs—but so does new life. Indeed, it's his thesis that these crashes are what have often set the stage for great advancement in the ecosystem as a whole. These crashes have produced the conditions for what can be called evolution in the created order. Fruitfulness came out of these apparent natural disasters.

Le Pichon, a devout Catholic, has also dedicated much of his life to caring for the mentally and physically disabled. He served with Mother Teresa's Missionaries of Charity in India as a young man and later came to live with handicapped people in group homes that are part of the L'Arche movement started by Jean Vanier in France in 1964. These communities have at their center people with profound limitations, weaknesses, and vulnerabilities. He also came to see that in the context of these communities, profound new life—and love—emerged by spending time with those who were limited in these ways, living with them, caring for them, and being cared for by them in surprising ways. He was changed by being in the constant presence of such vulnerable people. His heart was changed. He learned how to love. He came to have the courage to acknowledge where he was vulnerable, where he was weak and needed help. He also learned how to accept love on a deeper level. In the course of all these experiences, his heart became different. His heart *evolved*. He could see the commonality between what he observed in the created order at the deepest levels of the life of the earth in the dynamics of plate tectonics and what he came to experience personally in these Christian communities. There is something, he could see, at the very heart of natural and human reality that suggests that real life emerges when there is weakness at the center, when vulnerability arises and when things don't seem to *work*.

This "evolution" is possible in our daily lives too. This is what lies behind the aspect of the Morning Offering that God can be found if we seek him both in the good and in the bad—when things work well and when they fail, and when we are strong as well as when we are weak. St. Paul said that we in fact can *boast* about our weaknesses (see 2 Cor 12:8–10). Why? Because God has already united himself with them.

Areas in which we are weak give God a chance to show his strength there—to love us at our most vulnerable and in need and to let his glory shine exactly *right there*, through those spots that are broken down. This is, in fact, the central mystery of our Christian faith and what makes our understanding of God, the world, and our own lives so different. God has united himself to something that seems unfitting, namely, human weakness.

A Healing Encounter

The idea that somehow the most fragile parts of our lives and our hearts can be the most important, and potentially the most holy places comes from the gospels themselves. Again and again, it was those who were *desperate* to meet Jesus who came away healed and redeemed by that meeting.

Think of the blind man on the side of the road. As Jesus passes by, the man screams out, making quite a scene, "Son of David, have pity on me!" (Lk 18:35–43).

Or think of the guys carrying their buddy to the house where Jesus was teaching (see Mk 2:1–12). Right in the middle of Jesus' preaching, they break through the roof and lower their paralyzed friend down on a stretcher right before him. Talk about breaking protocol! This was not the way to approach God politely, but that's okay because God broke the rules first. God departed from what it means to be God by letting himself take on the limits of human nature. And because God acted this way first, we can have the boldness to act outside of the bounds of how we think we should act and speak when it comes to God.

Let's take a closer look at the case of the paralytic man who was lowered through the roof, which is rich in meaning on several levels. First, here is a man who is initiating nothing. It's the efforts of his friends that get him there. Secondly, there's something curious about his approaching Jesus from above, a kind of "condescension" (lowering himself in order to encounter the Lord). Early theologians typically attributed condescension to divinity, but here the man must be lowered even farther, exposing his friends to anger and ridicule for their actions. And in that place of lowliness, the man meets Jesus and is healed precisely there.

How about the woman at the well (see Jn 4:4–42)? She was going about her daily life, but Jesus found a way to get into the places of her heart and of her history where she most needed him whether she knew it or not. In the course of the dialogue between Jesus and her, some things were revealed that she did not want revealed, surely, but for which she ultimately needed healing. And once the shameful parts of her life were revealed to Jesus and his mercy, she went away, transformed. She became an evangelist. She went back to her village and told everyone, "You have to meet this one. He changes everything. He brings freedom!"

An Invitation

When I was a first-year novice, I remember getting some good advice. At that time we had spiritual direction every week. This was new to me, so we discussed what kinds of things come up in that context. My director told me that whatever I didn't want to talk about—because it seemed too embarrassing, it got us into territory that was too confusing, or I just didn't know how to talk about it—was *exactly* what should be talked about.

I think the same goes for personal prayer, and especially this simple prayer of the Morning Offering. "I offer you my joys and my sorrows, Lord" is not as innocuous or harmless as it seems at first. The more attentive we can be to what we need to surrender to the Lord, the more we dispose ourselves to receive what he wants to give us, precisely for our healing and for the fullness of life for us.

It helps if we can talk very specifically about this with Jesus in personal prayer. It's important to talk to him about not only what we're trying to do as we offer him our joys and sufferings but also what actually went on in the day. It is to that territory that we now turn in the "second moment" of prayer in daily life—remembering the day in the nightly Examen.

A Despair Prayer
St. Claude de la Colombiere, S.J.

> Lord, I am in this world to show your mercy to others.
> Other people will glorify you
> by making visible the power of your grace
> by their fidelity and constancy to you.
> For my part I will glorify you
> by making known how good you are to sinners,
> that your mercy is boundless
> and that no sinner no matter how great his offences
> should have reason to despair of pardon.
> If I have grievously offended you, my Redeemer,
> let me not offend you even more
> by thinking that you are not kind enough to pardon me.
> Amen.

Questions and Reflections

1. Remember a time when a loved one was suffering. What was it like to want to take some of that onto yourself instead?

2. How did the love between you get deeper as a result?

3. When have I been the one suffering while knowing that someone who loved me experienced a different kind of suffering because of it?

4. How might Jesus be looking upon your suffering or that of your loved one right now? What's in his Heart? Ask him.

PART II

The Examen

• • •

An Examen (at the end of the day)

Quiet yourself and rest in God's presence a few moments.

Thank God for a few concrete gifts of the day. Ask for light from the Holy Spirit to remember the day well.

Review the events of your day, from morning until now, even if for just a few moments. Pay attention to the movements of your heart. Notice where you are surprised and especially grateful for an encounter or experience and where you are ashamed of how you acted in a particular circumstance.

Thank God again for the good memories. Ask for forgiveness for the bad ones.

Rest in God's presence a few moments more. Ask for the grace of a peaceful sleep and for the gift of being open-hearted again when you wake up.

The Power of Remembering

• • •

Remember that you too were once slaves in Egypt, and the LORD, your God, brought you from there with his strong hand and outstretched arm.

—Deuteronomy 5:15

An old Jesuit psychiatrist once quipped to me, "A decent nap can turn one bad day into two good ones." After a little rest, a person is likely to be more ready and attentive for what comes along later. When one is rested and ready for the "second day," the irritability factor diminishes, patience increases, and the capacity to be grateful for the gifts that would be given grows.

But what about the "first day"? There's something about being refreshed enough to *remember* well what happened earlier in the day that makes that memory seem better, richer, and more *real*. Simply remembering what has already happened and how God has already been active in one's day makes the soul more attentive to God's presence and care in ordinary, day-to-day living.

The use of memory in prayer is essential for developing a sense of what is true and real. Though our relationship with the Lord is always in the *present*, we want to be able to bring the fullness of who we are, including all that we have experienced in the *past*, into the *present* of our relationship with the Lord. And when we bring the past into dialogue with the Lord, the past, in a very real way, gets redeemed. The unfolding of the story of our daily lives is given a new coherence. Our memories can be healed. And when our history looks redeemed, the possibilities of our futures also start to seem new, and we can move forward with new confidence.

In order for the Examen to bear fruit in our lives, we must consider carefully not only the events of the day—good and bad—but our thoughts and impressions about what happened as well. In the next two chapters, we will take a closer look at how to discern these things. For now, let's take a closer look at how the Morning Offering and evening Examen, together, help us live with greater intentionality and awareness in the Heart of Christ.

The Second Moment: The Examen

As you begin to incorporate the three moments into your daily prayer, it may help you to think about the first and second moments as the "bookends" of each day, to keep our spiritual vision both lofty and grounded. (Please note that the third moment of daily prayer, the celebration of the Eucharist, draws up into itself what pertains both to the Morning Offering and to the Examen—the idealism and the realism that marks our life in Christ. Therefore, we use this "bookends" approach, rather than exploring each moment in chronological order.)

We refer to the Morning Offering and Examen as "bookends" because there are many ways to approach God in prayer throughout the day. St. Ignatius encouraged a complete array of different kinds of prayer within his work, the Spiritual Exercises. He urges us to pray by looking at the beauty of nature, by reading scripture, by using our imaginations to encounter the Lord more personally within scripture, and by reciting rote prayers including the Our Father, the Hail Mary, and the Anima Christi. He also encouraged praying in informal conversation, such as chatting with the Father, Jesus, and Mary about what is going on in our lives. He calls these chats "colloquies," meaning simply "speaking with." He practiced all of these forms of prayer and saw the good in all of them at different times in his life.

Yet, above all other forms of prayer, Ignatius thought the Examen was especially useful in daily life. He told the Jesuits in his charge that even if they got so busy during the day that the other forms of prayer fell by the wayside, they must not let the Examen go. It is the essential prayer for "finding God in all things and all things in God." The Examen brings together all the threads of the day to see what actually happened in light of that hoped-for union with Christ's Heart.

I think what's great about the Examen is that one does not need extraordinary focus, concentration, or mental discipline to do it. Sometimes praying can seem so daunting, as if only the experts or saints really know how to do it right. Prayer can seem esoteric and only for people that are already on their way to leading perfect lives—that isn't me! Ordinary people like me get nervous that we'll do it wrong and miss something. To break this block, sometimes we have to psyche ourselves up to do something as dramatic as to *pray*. Sometimes I don't have the energy for that, at least not every day.

The Examen is a way of prayer in which we simply *remember* things that happened during the day in the presence of God. We just spend a few minutes answering questions such as these: What happened today? Whom did I meet? What feelings did I have? What did I go through? How did I act and react to people and to situations? But the most important question is this one: what happened to my *heart* today?

In the "first moment" we talked about making a simple prayer of offering at the beginning of the day: "Jesus, I want to live with my heart united to your heart today, opened up to the world, able to be pierced and yet remaining on fire." Now here at the end of the day, I simply want to review what actually happened. In the morning I made an offering. I set out an ideal for myself. Now in this evening review, I look back to see how that offering went. When did I give my heart away, and when I did I start to take it back?

It's important that in the Examen, our reflection is different from an examination of conscience. We are not recalling the day merely to accuse ourselves of sins and failures. Furthermore, we are not talking to *ourselves* about the day – that would not be very helpful. Talking to someone else about it is much better. Talking to God about it is best! While we remember things in God's presence, our sins and failures might very well come up, and the technique of the Examen gives us a strategy to deal with them, a different perspective.

Our Christian vision is that we *can* become perfect. We do not pray the Examen seeking perfection on our own. The Examen isn't a self-help technique. We will not get more perfect on our own. We grow in perfection only to the degree that we remain in friendship with God.

The Examen is a chance to talk over the day with a friend. God became human in order to be our friend. Through this friendship, we become more like Jesus, and we become better people—more loving, more honest, wiser, and humbler.

The Examen takes us along the way to Christian perfection but not as a private project. In the Examen we remember the day, not alone, but *with* God: telling stories; trying to remember details; getting help from others to get it right; and being happy somehow when the story gets told and remembered—together. In making the Examen, we recall each day lived with God, precisely because Jesus has lived the same day with his heart opened up to each one of us.

Getting the Story Right

I've been blessed to be born into a family that tells stories all the time. Being more Irish than anything else doesn't hurt in this regard, I suppose. But I'm guessing a lot of families do the same. We tell stories. And the stories get better, the memories more vivid, the more those stories are brought into relationship. It makes for a good party, of course, when the stories start rolling.

My Maloney cousins come from Tyler, Texas, which—as everybody knows—is where the best storytellers come from. I have eight cousins from that family, one girl and seven boys, each one bigger than the next, and their dad was bigger than them all. We call their mom Aunt Biddy. Her kids get their storytelling ability from her as much as from their dad.

To one family gathering at the Maloney's house, one of my cousins brought a new girlfriend. As things got going, Aunt Biddy launched into one of her stories, flicking the long ash from her Lark cigarette, a Weller's bourbon on the rocks within easy reach. (These are essential ingredients to Aunt Biddy's storytelling process.)

Aunt Biddy had just begun laying the foundations of her story when the visiting girlfriend leaned over discreetly and indicated to Aunt Biddy that she had already told that story. No doubt she was trying to be considerate and didn't want Aunt Biddy to embarrass herself.

A hush came over the crowd. Everyone knew full well that Aunt Biddy had already told the story, and recently too, but that didn't matter in the least. In fact, everyone wanted to hear it again precisely *because* they had already heard it. What else are you going to do at a Maloney family party?

There's something very satisfying about telling our stories over and over again, especially with family, and also with friends. Through the storytelling, through the common remembering, we are reconstituted. We are made again. In an amazing way, communal remembering gives us back our identities in a new way. Our shared history gives us a way to go forward. We need to recall our stories, for our whole life is one story in progress. Married couples tell their stories when they celebrate their anniversaries. Each year, usually on the Feast of St. Ignatius, Jesuits in formation formally renew their vows. On that occasion we recall the stories of Ignatius's life and our own and how they had been wound up together in the common call we have of following Christ.

Of course we tell stories in church every time we go to Mass. We hear the same old stories. But it's not the same old experience. If we listen, the stories strike us in new ways every time we hear them. They help us remember who we truly are. We get to know our history, our family, and our God who has mixed himself up in this messy history of ours. And when we hear the stories, we are made new again. In the hearing, in the remembering, we are given the boost to keep going with confidence into an uncertain future.

By remembering the stories of a particular day in the company of our God, the Examen also helps us to keep going with confidence into the uncertain future.

A New Day in Remembering

As modest a prayer effort as is the Examen, it's surprisingly fruitful. Even if all you can do is five or ten minutes at the end of the day, try it and see what happens. If you're like me, you'll be amazed at how rich the day becomes when you're looking back on it with the Lord.

The Examen is a good antidote to our tendency to fall into ruts and feel that all our days are the same. Before an Examen, we can have a day that seems just a blur of activity and undistinguished encounters. When I apply the gift of memory to the day, through the Examen, the day becomes sharper, clearer, and much more meaningful. Even when I take these few moments at the end of the day to do nothing more than remember, I am usually amazed by how much actually did happen, how rich the day actually was. Without this act of remembering, all the little moments of beauty, joy, fun, and interesting things can all just fall off the radar because we were so focused on moving on to the next thing.

Here's the most astonishing thing to me: When I remember, it's as if the day itself becomes different. When I remember the day, it changes. And in my experience, the day changes for the better as I share it with the Lord, not for the worse, every time. I come away from every Examen more grateful for the day. The gratitude happens on its own, not because I'm trying to *make* myself more grateful. It's just that remembering, as I've said, makes us see more clearly life as a whole, how it's all put

together, and how it makes up one coherent story even if there's
a lot of mess in the midst of it.

How to Do an Examen

What I've just described is a way of remembering the day as a
whole in the broadest terms. St. Ignatius gave an outline of steps
for this remembering. Here's the plan.

1. *Give thanks.* Quickly find something from the day, anything, for which you are grateful. It might be the jelly donut you
had for breakfast, the fact that we finally got some sunshine after
days of rain, or the call you received from an old friend. Maybe
you will recall many things you can be thankful for. Regardless
of the objects, the recognition of gratitude puts us in a disposi-
tion to be able to receive what the Lord has to show us in these
next few moments.

2. *Ask for light from the Holy Spirit.* Asking for light is an act
of humility. When we do it, we are recognizing that there might
be more to this past day than we think there is. When we place
ourselves under the guidance of the Holy Spirit, more will be
revealed—the good and the bad alike. We will be able to see
more clearly the gifts in our lives as well as how ungrateful and
selfish we might have been. By the light of the Holy Spirit, we
will be moved simultaneously to both gratitude and repentance.
Afterward we will desire to be more grateful and humble in the
future.

3. *Give an account.* This step is at the heart of the Examen.
Here, we take a bird's-eye view of the day that has just passed.
If we are doing this in the evening, as many find convenient,
we can begin the review from the time we woke up. Or maybe
we take it from the last time we did the review, sometime the

previous day. Regardless of where you start, it's good to remember about a twenty-four-hour stretch of time.

So what are we looking for? We do not need to look at *every detail* of the day. What is important is what catches our attention *affectively*, emotionally. What things happened that I feel in my gut? What movements in your heart did you experience? These movements of the spirit are the most important things to attend to. The Holy Spirit brings to mind those things in our day that are spiritually important. The movements indicate where the action is. They reveal what is important for our relationship with God, for our ongoing conversion, and therefore ultimately for our happiness, so we can live life to the fullest, as Jesus wants us to do.

For example, maybe this past day I took a big exam or I gave a big presentation at work that had worried me for weeks. But now when I look back on the day, it might well be that the actual experience of the exam or presentation doesn't stir much of anything in my heart. Instead, perhaps it's an encounter with a stranger at the grocery store who irritated me by pushing ahead of me in the checkout line. Or maybe I recall a brief exchange with someone in the hallway who offered to me a simple kindness that now, when I look back on it, I realize really lifted my spirit. So in my Examen, I'm now moved by gratitude for those few words of kindness. And while I'm at it, I will consider how I felt and now feel about the stranger in the grocery store who irritated me. What matters is the *movement* of my heart, and these movements sometimes do not involve the big events of our lives as we might predict.

The thing to remember about doing the Examen is that you and I can get caught off guard. In fact, I am almost always surprised by what comes up. Most important, when I look at the day in the presence of the Lord, I'm continually amazed by how much beauty has been operative even though I took no time to recognize it or savor it until now.

4. *Repent for harm done.* While an Examen is not the same as an examination of conscience, as I look back on the day and do the inventory in the presence of Jesus, I simply have to have the courage to acknowledge my sin to the Lord and humble myself to ask forgiveness.

To acknowledge where I have sinned is part of what goes on in the Examen, and yet an Examen is not to be confused with an examination of conscience. As I remember the day, my memory will certainly present to me plain, old sinful actions to which I must plead guilty. And I will feel a movement in my spirit of guilt and regret when I recall these actions. However, the Examen attempts to review every moment of the day and allow the more subtle agitations to emerge.

I might ask myself:

- What were the movements of my heart that preceded these events?

- What strong emotions emerged in these moments? Did I start to feel sorry for myself, or get scared about a situation? Did I experience an unexpected sense of joy or peace?

- How did a particular moment of the day "set me up" for things that I later did or said? Did these interior feelings of self-pity or fear, for example, set me up to later do what is sinful to another—to lash out, to gossip, or to be judgmental? Did the feeling of isolation earlier in the day set me up to drink too much later or tempt me to waste time escaping through the Internet?

If I am doing this every day, I start to recognize with more subtlety what needs to be brought to the sacrament of Reconciliation—to confession—later on in the month, perhaps. This act of humility, of recognizing where I turned in on myself, is itself an act of being united to the Heart of Christ. I am letting my own heart be opened up by a kind of piercing truth of my own selfishness. When I do open up in this way to Jesus, he has a chance to come close to me where I most need him, where he most wants to heal me, to forgive me, and to bring me back into his friendship.

5. *Ask for help tomorrow.* In reviewing my day, I've noticed some things to be grateful for. Living my days in gratitude tends to make me more humble, more joyful, and easier to be around. Think of the people you know who are grateful. Now think of the ones who are always complaining. With whom do you naturally want to spend time? There's extra motivation for us in taking up this practice of the Examen.

In addition to this infusion of gratitude, my review also brings to light things that need help. I always remember things I regret or feel guilty about. In the presence of the Lord, I have to be honest about these things. I can't blame everyone else for what goes wrong in my life; I must own up to my part of the mess. And as I take responsibility for what is disordered in my life, I am also setting myself up for improvement and growth in the future. For example, if I know that I am likely to get judgmental and snarky when I get around that particular friend of mine, or that I will get defensive and petty when I go into that staff meeting because I feel insecure there, I am coming to know specifically where I need help and where Jesus wants to be with me. I am coming to know, in very ordinary ways, where I need redemption and where I need healing.

Only Jesus can provide the healing and redemption we need in our deepest being. By letting him in on these not-so-pretty areas of my life, of my heart, and of my history, he has a chance to take over and allow something new to happen in me. I'm not stuck anymore with my own self, my own stale history, and my own boring and exhausting patterns of sin. After I have remembered what has gone on today, I am more disposed tomorrow to somehow let the Lord in where I need him most.

As I'm writing this, for example, I keep thinking of an exchange I had three days ago. I was driving back from Sunday Masses at a parish in St. Louis. As I got off the highway and came up to a stoplight at the end of the exit ramp, there was a man begging for money at the curb right next to my car. In the part of St. Louis where I live, this kind of thing happens quite a bit, and I'm sorry to say I usually just shut down when I come across someone in these circumstances. If I'm walking, I can pretend that I'm busy and tell the person I'm sorry but I don't have anything to give him or her.

This time, probably because I was trapped in my car and wearing my Roman collar, I was forced into having to respond more personally. I grudgingly made eye contact, rolled down the window, and reached into my pocket for a dollar to give the man. He thanked me, and then we just started talking (St. Louis has long red lights!). It was the first nice spring day we had had coming out of winter, and it was opening day for the Cardinals. We both commented on the weather and on our hopes for the baseball season ahead. Then the light turned green. I said good-bye and drove off.

So I ask myself, *Why am I remembering this story again, three days later?* I think it's the Lord's way of showing me that my heart is longing for more of those simple human interactions.

I am so busy in my work for the Church and the university that I tend to shut out these personal interactions when they present themselves. I believe the Holy Spirit is telling me to start opening up a bit more and just be in the present with the people I happen to come across. That's where life is. And continuing along the path of moving quickly past people to do "more important" things—that's a path to death!

Remembering Together

The fruitfulness of praying the Examen is twofold. The remembering is key, but equally essential is that the remembering takes place in the context of relationship. Specifically, the remembering takes place in relationship to God who has entered into history and become a person. From the moment of the Incarnation, all of creation, all of humanity, and all of history—including my own—has become a part of God's life. My life is now within God's life, my story within God's story.

This ongoing cultivation of relationship is seen over and over again in the lives of the saints. St. Augustine spent his youth and much of his adult life wandering physically, intellectually, morally, and spiritually. After his conversion to Christ, he expressed a sense of wonder about his relationship with God. Augustine realized that his whole life had been taking place *within* the God who is Love, who is himself in relationship with the Father, Son, and Holy Spirit. That realization shed light on his past, present, and future.

Pope Benedict highlighted the truth of a Christian's relationship with God in a homily he gave in the context of baptismal celebrations. He noted that when we are baptized, we are plunged into God's very *self*—into the name and very identity of God. In the rite of Baptism, the priest or deacon, standing in for Christ, first asks the child's name. Then, with the pouring or immersion into water, the priest or deacon "plunges" that little person into the reality of God, into those divine relationships, essentially by saying something such as, "Elizabeth, I baptize you into the name of God—into the Father, Son, and Holy Spirit." At Baptism, we were inserted into the memory of God. Our story was inserted into the one story of God.

An Invitation

From the moment of Baptism, God the Father calls us his beloved sons and daughters. When Jesus went down under the waters of the Jordan River at his own Baptism, he came up and heard the Father say, by the power of the Holy Spirit, "You are my beloved Son. In you I am well pleased." We went into those waters of the Jordan, too, when we were baptized.

Ever since then, the Father has been saying the same thing to us: "You are my beloved daughter. You are my beloved son. In you I am well pleased." This is who we are. This is the one story that makes sense of all other stories in our lives. This is the story we have to be reminded of every day. The Examen helps us to do just that. But it gets hard to hear that truth clearly, in our hearts. We are going to turn now to look at what some of those difficulties are and how we can work to keep the ears of our hearts open so that we can hear the Father saying, "You are my beloved. In you I am well pleased."

Ever Ancient, Ever New
St. Augustine of Hippo

Late have I loved you, O Beauty so ancient and so new, late have I loved you! Lo, you were within but I outside, seeking there for you, and upon the shapely things you have made, I rushed headlong, I, misshapen, you were with me but I was not with you. They held me back far from you, those things which would have no being were they not in you. You called, shouted, broke through my deafness; You flared, blazed, banished my blindness; You lavished your fragrance; I gasped and now I pant for you; I have tasted you and I hunger and thirst; you touched me, and I burned for your peace.

Questions and Reflections

1. What in my personal history has been wounded? Can I let the Holy Spirit help me to remember those wounds right now? How can that history come into the present?

2. What in my heart, in my history, needs healing? Ask Jesus to remember those wounds with you. How was he with you when you experienced that hurt originally? Maybe first ask Mary to remember with you. Ask her what was in her heart as you were going through that difficulty.

3. In the more immediate past, such as today, what happened that was difficult or painful? When did I say something or do something that was destructive or small hearted? Let Jesus in on that more recent memory.

4. When was the last time I went to confession? Make a point to bring that to confession for forgiveness and healing—soon!

Who Are You Talking To?

• • •

The Pharisee took up his position and spoke this prayer to himself, "O God, I thank you that I am not like the rest of humanity—greedy, dishonest, adulterous—or even like this tax collector. I fast twice a week, and I pay tithes on my whole income." But the tax collector stood off at a distance and would not even raise his eyes to heaven but beat his breast and prayed, "O God, be merciful to me a sinner."

—Luke 18:11–13

How often do you talk to yourself? When you're going through the day, in those times by yourself, do you have little monologues going on in your head? I have a good Jesuit friend who does a lot of spiritual direction; he suggested that when I am feeling angry or tense or bad in any way, I stop and ask myself, "Who am I talking to?" It's simple, but it's incredibly helpful.

Here's what I find: When I'm feeling crummy, I try to get a sense of what I am saying to myself, especially when I find myself repeating the same thing over and over. Sometimes I'm talking about other people, casting various kinds of judgments on them, rehearsing what I should have said to them when they said that mean or hurtful thing to me. I can spend a lot of time working on good, cutting, and clever comebacks. Unfortunately, it's too late for comebacks. I'll never be able to go back to that conversation with the person who hurt me. And the longer I keep reliving that moment in the past, the more resentful and deflated I become. The enemy is winning when this happens. I'm falling right into the trap he has set for me when I get stuck in the past like that.

Other times when I get caught up in this inner monologue, I realize I'm talking to myself about the future: what I'm going to say to that person the next time he speaks to me and how I might get back at that one. I might even be wishing something bad might happen to that person! These monologues can get pretty dark, if I'm honest with myself.

In my experience, though, the most destructive monologues going on inside of me are the ones that are focused not on others but on me. In my monologues, I am most likely to be muttering to myself *about myself*. I talk to myself specifically about my failures and my inadequacies, the things I'm ashamed of or feel discouraged about. The enemy is strong here too. Whether I'm making judgments to myself about others or about myself, the enemy has me just where he wants me—in isolation, in a spirit of accusation, and in a mode of berating, causing deflation, discouragement, fear, and anxiety.

Tell Me the Truth!

In the last chapter, we ended with a brief discussion about what happens in Baptism and, specifically, what gets said in Baptism. The Father calls each one of us, from that point on, his beloved daughter or his beloved son. That's the bottom-line truth of who we are. Yet, we can't just tell *ourselves* that we are beloved of God. That doesn't work. It only works when we *hear* God say it to us.

We are most our true selves, most who we are created to be, when we are *listening*—listening to others around us, yes, but ultimately listening to God, particularly God the Father. This is one way of looking at the essence of Jesus' whole mission. He comes to be one of us to draw us close so that we can hear in our hearts, at the depths of who we are, what the Father has to say to us.

Hearing What Jesus Hears

Try this little prayer exercise the next time you have a little extra time: Get yourself settled in a quiet place. Then ask the Holy Spirit for help to see and to hear. Recall the scene of the Baptism of Jesus in the Jordan (see Mk 1:2–13). Consider all those people gathered down at the river to listen to John and to be baptized into his "baptism of repentance." He was a radical preacher, calling people back from a life of sin. Recall that he was a stark figure, radical not only in his preaching but also in his lifestyle: dwelling in the desert, dressing in animal hides, eating locusts, and so on. Getting the picture? The Baptist was a wild man from all outward appearances!

Now consider all those people who dropped everything to go listen to him and be baptized by him. This must have been a motley crew, gathered by that little river trickling through the desert, looking for hope in such a bleak setting. These were not well-groomed, sophisticated, well-adjusted people who were comfortable in their place in the world. Most likely they were on the fringes of society for one reason or another. For many, it had to have been their last chance personally, emotionally, and spiritually.

Then Jesus shows up, the "light to the nations" foretold by the likes of Anna and Simeon. This is the messiah, the anointed one who was sent to deliver the people of God from their enemies, the Son of the Most High who is to sit on the throne of David, whose kingdom will have no end. And this one, the one whom we know to be God in the flesh, comes down to this rugged spot in the Jordan, to be with these desperate people and begin his mission here. He chose this setting.

John hesitates, feeling the inappropriateness of the encounter. Jesus is ready to go down under the water, in an act of humility and of letting go of power and influence. But before he goes down, hear him call you by your name. He is asking you to come down from the riverbank where you have been watching at a safe distance until now. Let Jesus call you by name. Now you go down into the water to join him. Let him show you how to descend, how to go low, and how to get small.

While you're there under the water, stay there for a while. Let yourself go. Start to empty out. Whatever it is that you're worried about, let that come out of your heart and flow downriver. Whatever it is that you're ashamed of, let that flow away. Whatever it is that you're proud of, whatever your skills, talents, or accomplishments, let those go too. Whatever it is that you are clinging to, let go. Let go of all the resentments and anger that you cling to. Let go of the aspects of your identity that you want everyone to see, that make you feel worthwhile. Let them all go. Empty everything out until you have nothing left.

Now you're ready to let Jesus show you how to come up out of that water.

As you come up, take in the silence and the emptiness. Into that silence and emptiness, you hear a word. The Father speaks from above, saying to Jesus and through Jesus to you: "You are my beloved son. You are my beloved daughter. In you I am well pleased."

Respond to the Father

When the Father speaks, try to just listen. He calls you his beloved child. How does that feel? Does it move you? Are you consoled? Are you surprised by the love coming into your heart? Do you feel different? Perhaps it makes you feel anxious. Do you wish those words were true, but they ring hollow for you? Are you saddened to hear what you wish were true but believe is not the case? Perhaps you feel nothing. Are you numb and saddened by your numbness?

How do you start to respond? What do you start to say? Maybe, if the words are getting into your heart, there is nothing to say. Maybe you stay silent in gratitude and joy beyond words and you don't want to leave this moment.

Or maybe you say to yourself something like this: *I wish it were true that I was the beloved, and I think probably at one time, I might have been but not anymore. I blew that opportunity. I have so screwed things up in my life, in my relationships, and with God that those days of being beloved are just gone.* Or perhaps you're a little more optimistic, thinking, *Maybe I could be the beloved again, if I got my act together. If I worked harder and was kinder or did some better things with my life, maybe the Father would call me his beloved. But I'd better get to work. I have some improving to do!*

If you start talking to yourself like this, even though these words seem like humble, even holy, things to say, you should know that the enemy has already weaseled his way back in, dividing you from the Lord ever so subtly and tempting you to lie even to the Lord, who sees everything: "Well thanks for saying that, Father, but you're not really right about that. You've actually got it wrong. I appreciate the sentiment, but you're a bit off base. I'll tell you what, I'll get back to you when I have things worked out better, when I really am worthy of being your beloved."

When we "pray" like this, we are telling God he is wrong. Think about that. Let it sink in. We are telling God the Father, the Creator of the world, the one who has no beginning and no end, and the one who knitted each of us together in our mothers' wombs—in the presence of his Son—that he, God, is in fact wrong. Not a good place to be.

Instead of telling God what's what, maybe we should let him do the talking, and we can do the listening. Make no mistake; you and I are the beloved of the Father. Even in the face of our very real selfishness and sinfulness, he speaks through that and underneath it, as it were. He speaks the truth through all the lies that we have fallen for, all the lies that we have told, and all the lies that we have come to believe. The Father says, "You are my beloved. In you I am well pleased. Right now."

Getting to the Root of the Truth

God always speaks in the present. The enemy tries to distract us with the past or the future, but God the Father is in this very moment speaking love to my heart and to yours.

The enemy likes it when we get stuck. Sometimes we are paralyzed by our shame or the past: *Why did I mess that up? What was I thinking? How could I have been so stupid, so selfish?* Other times, it's our fear of the future: *I'm really going to do better. I'm going to fix this. I'm going to get it right—who am I kidding? I'll never get it right. My chance has passed. I'm a loser. Nobody is going to love me now. Face it: I am unlovable. Nobody wants me. Beloved? Hah! Get real.*

This is the battle we're in. The Father is always speaking to us through his Holy Spirit and in our relationship with his Son in the Church. He's always telling us the truth. And the enemy is always lying to us, trying to isolate us. Sometimes there's a grain of truth in those lies. I did mess things up. It will be hard to do better in the future. But the truth of what the Father says must not get obscured by the grains of the truth within those big lies from the enemy.

The only way the past can be healed and the only way I can have confidence for the future is if I let God speak first. And I listen. If I let into my heart what the Father is saying, and if I do *get* that I am loved by the Father, then I will live in truth, and when I live in truth, I become free.

So we know the truth. The truth is, we are in relationship, loved by the Father. That's not just an idea that we acknowledge once and then everything will be fine. It's a truth that has to be lived every day. And to live in this truth, we should use the gift of memory. We've got to remember the truth, and we've also got to recognize when we have fallen into listening to lies and then to reject those lies. To grow in our relationship with God, we need to pay attention to these dynamics every day.

Talking through Hurt

We're probably all familiar, either directly or indirectly, with the experience of suffering through divorce. The initial experience of the breakup is bad enough, but the collateral damage to relationships within the family continue to make problems, even years later.

For those going through this, it is tempting to live in dread of the future. People worry about their children and the possibility of losing them. As parents, they worry that the mistakes they made, both as spouses and as parents, will forever damage their relationships with their children.

Of course, such concerns are understandable. They can also become fixations. We can start to cling to them. Clinging to reasons to worry or to trains of thought can lead us to fear, isolation, and paralysis. Sound familiar? This is exactly where the enemy wants us—believing these *lies*.

It is essential for people in this situation to keep on talking, to articulate their fears and doubts, and then remember together—in dialogue with a friend or with the Lord—what the truth is. Remember together what the true story is. We can help a friend or a loved one who is slipping into the paralysis of these lies: "That's not the story! You need a new narrative!"

Sometimes painful experiences tempt us to lose perspective, to think that everything is going against us: *My life is over since I went through this divorce. If I had married somebody better, I never would have had these problems. It's my own fault. I should have known better. I deserve this pain. Here I am, and now my life is pretty much doomed. I'm going to be poor forever. My kids will be messed up. They'll never forgive me. They'll always love my ex more than me. Nobody else will love me. My life will be misery from here on out. It is what it is: defeat.*

When it comes to dealing with past hurts, doing a daily Examen can help a great deal to sort out what's what. By clearly remembering who I am before God as beloved son or daughter, I can go forward with examining the day. I can remember the day in light of the bigger story. When I register in the movements of my heart and in the thoughts that run through my head what sounds like it comes from the enemy, things that lead me into fear, anxiety, isolation, or discouragement, I can reject those things—or at least realize that something entered my day that caused me to lose sight of the truth. Then I can situate myself in the larger picture and remember the true narrative.

When we do this kind of remembering, it's important to remember that we are not just trying to convince ourselves of a happier reality. This whole spirituality and way of praying in daily life is not a way of trying to make a new, more desirable narrative. No, it is an attempt to open our eyes to the narrative that actually exists. The story within which we are living is the story of Jesus and the paschal mystery—his life, death, and resurrection. That story is the basis of reality itself. Whatever it is that we're going through at any time, it is happening within the story of Jesus.

Jesus himself taught us to pray like this when he introduced his disciples to the Our Father: "Thy kingdom come, thy will be done on earth as it is in heaven" and "Give us this day our daily bread." These phrases acknowledge the truth that my little life is taking place in the context of a larger life, that it is happening within divine life.

Reflecting on the Lord's Prayer, Pope Benedict said, "When we pray the Our Father . . . we ask the Lord that 'your will be done, on earth as it is in heaven.' In other words, we recognize that God has a will for us and with us, that God has a will for our lives. Each day this must increasingly become the reference point for our desires and our existence."[7]

Each day of our own lives is a day within the divine life, and if we are to know how to live tomorrow, we must be reminding ourselves where we are in the story.

Walking the Via Crucis

A few years ago I had the privilege of joining a group of young adults for a pilgrimage to the Holy Land. Every day was full of incredible grace, to be able to witness the key places in the history of our salvation and to do so with a group with such lively faith.

On the last full day in Jerusalem, the culmination of the pilgrimage, we made the Stations of the Cross along the *Via Dolorosa*, which winds through the markets of the Old City, and then entered the Church of the Holy Sepulchre to celebrate Mass on the spot that tradition holds to be the place where Jesus was nailed to the Cross on Good Friday. It is impossible for me to describe how humbling that was and how grateful I remain for the opportunity.

An even deeper grace caught me off guard shortly after the Mass, bringing together for me this whole mystery of *remembering the story*. When we finished Mass, our guide showed us various nooks and crannies within the Church of the Holy Sepulchre, which included the place where Jesus' body was lain before it was placed in the tomb as well as the tomb itself. There was also a nondescript space *below* the area marking the place of the crucifixion, a little cave carved out of the small hill on which the crucifixion took place.

According to one legend, this cave is referred to as the place of "Adam's tomb," recalling the first man created out of love and the first to sin. This cave, then, bears witness to the "wages" of that first sin (see Rom 6:23). This cave is the place of original death.

And so if we consider this whole scene of the place of Jesus' crucifixion and the tomb of Adam below it, the life-giving blood from the Heart of Christ flows from the Cross through hardened layers of rock and human history until it reaches the original figure of human history, redeeming him and lifting him up from death into new life, to share in the Resurrection. The deepest, darkest, and most fossilized area of human history is precisely where the blood of Christ penetrates, redeems, and restores. In a powerful way, I was reminded that Christ's love and self-sacrifice not only is our hope for the future but also redeems the past. That's what we believe. This is the story of every human creature since the beginning of time—not just for Adam but for all of us.

A Reflection

Imagine standing there beside me at that place of original death of Adam. Reflect upon your own history for a moment. Is there one place in your heart, in your history, that is a place of "original death" for you? Is there one deep wound in your life that needs that healing flow?

Did someone hurt you? Is this hurt a cause of resentment and anger? Or maybe, strangely, you feel guilt for what was done to you.

Or did you do the hurting? Is there one grave sin in your history that continues to linger and bring shame?

Perhaps the place of your original death is not the result of anyone hurting or being hurt on a moral level but rather simply the loss of a loved one. Is there the grief of loss that has hardened your heart? Does it seem impossible to love or to hope since that loss?

I suggest that this original death, this continuing pain, is the place in your life, your heart, and your history that you most need to open up to the blood of Christ, to the love of Christ. Just like that body of Adam, decaying in that cave for millennia, is being redeemed by the blood of Christ seeping through the layers of all human history, so too that blood, that love, flows from his Heart, seeking out your heart to bring it back to life.

Healing the "Core Wound"

Do you already know that place of original death, the "core wound" in need of healing? If you're unsure, think about the patterns of sin or self-destructive behavior you've noticed in yourself—or that have been brought to your attention. (If you go to confession on a regular basis, such patterns might be easier to identify.) Ask yourself, *Why do I keep doing this? Why do I keep falling into that same old trap?*

Doing an Examen on a daily basis also allows these patterns emerge: *Do I keep falling into the same old traps of gossip, judgmental attitudes, anger, or defensiveness? Do I act superior or "snotty," or try to find fault in others before they find it in me?*

Is it possible I do things such as this because I sense, deep down in my inner "core," that things aren't right? Do I believe that I'm not loved, that I'm not lovable? Do I believe that, if people only knew me, they would reject me?

That's where history comes into play. Identifying the wound I keep operating out of helps me to know where to let Jesus in, to heal me with a kind of divine "blood transfusion," with his new love flowing into me so that my heart starts to work better.

Letting Jesus in on what hurts and where the wounds are, on a daily basis, is good for the heart, freeing me to love better and to be happier. I just need to speak out to him what needs to be spoken from my own heart.

When I do that daily Examen, I will remember certain times in the day:

- times when I felt free and self-forgetful—full of joy and confidence;

- times when I wasn't self-preoccupied, or alternatively, when I got turned in on myself; and

- times when I got anxious, afraid, petty, jealous, envious, and lustful.

All these are expressions of turning in on myself in order to nurse those wounds that are irritating my heart. When I nurse those wounds with more sin, more self-preoccupation, things only get worse. What I need to do instead is to let Jesus into those areas. I just need to talk about these things with him.

At the beginning of the chapter, I suggested telling Jesus about that inner monologue in our heads and to expose the ridiculousness of what the enemy is getting us to fixate on. But as you go deeper, perhaps you will discover a "core wound" in your life. It is important to talk to Jesus about that in prayer. Expose that wound to him again and again for healing.

This is the purpose of the sacrament of Reconciliation. It helps to have a regular confessor who can track your progress and be helpful for facilitating the encounter with Jesus in an ever more particular and precise way.

Spiritual direction can also help a great deal in this process. But even in the absence of a regular confessor or a spiritual director, personal prayer and the sacrament of Reconciliation are great helps toward the healing and redeeming encounter with Jesus. When we go deeper and we know what needs to happen in our daily spiritual lives, we learn how to invite Jesus into what is going on and we become more and more familiar with the deceits of the enemy. We know his voice of accusation and discouragement. And we can learn to reject that voice as that of the Prince of Lies. If we know he's a liar, then why would we keep listening to him?

An Invitation

In the next chapter, we'll look more closely at what St. Ignatius calls the Rules for Discernment of Spirits. The Examen is the essential tool for bringing to the surface what needs to be dealt with in this spiritual battle that we are all in, whether we know it or not. When we notice areas of life and death, confidence and discouragement, and large-heartedness and small-heartedness, we know that the Holy Spirit is operating. And yet, we know that the enemy is also at work, accusing and distracting us in order to prevent that healing.

Identifying the "core wound" or place of "original death" in our lives gives us a great advantage. We know what's vulnerable and therefore where most of "the action" is in our spiritual lives. The spirit of Jesus wants to enter that vulnerable area in order to redeem it. The enemy also wants to go there, to exploit it, and to make that vulnerable place a cause of shame, further discouragement, and ultimately isolation from God. We need not cooperate with that exploitation. We can be free. But the only way to become free is to start listening to the truth.

Prayer of Abandonment
St. Charles de Foucauld

> Father,
> I abandon myself into your hands;
> do with me what you will.
> Whatever you may do, I thank you:
> I am ready for all, I accept all.
> Let only your will be done in me,
> and in all your creatures—
> I wish no more than this, O Lord.
> Into your hands I commend my soul:
> I offer it to you with all the love of my heart,
> for I love you, Lord, and so need to give myself,
> to surrender myself into your hands without reserve,
> and with boundless confidence,
> for you are my Father.

Questions and Reflections

1. When you are really feeling ornery during the day, stop and ask yourself what you're muttering about in your head.

2. What is that monologue going on in me? Am I addressing God or myself?

3. What judgments am I making about others? What judgments am I making about myself?

4. Now, don't change one word of what you're saying, but tell Jesus instead of yourself. Does it sound ridiculous? Does it just not sound accurate? Turn the monologue into a dialogue.

5. Have a laugh with him about what you were saying, first off. Now ask him what the truth of the situation is. You can only know the truth in dialogue—especially with Jesus.

Discernment of Spirits

· · ·

At once the Spirit drove him out into the desert,

and he remained in the desert for forty days, tempted by Satan.

He was among wild beasts, and the angels ministered to him.

—Mark 1:12–13

In the beginning of the Spiritual Exercises, St. Ignatius presents a series of exercises designed to help us identify disordered attachments. By "disordered attachments," Ignatius means whatever I am clinging to that holds me back in my relationship with the Lord. When we are liberated from these various attachments, we can become better able to know and do the will of God.

Practicing the Examen goes a long way toward helping us determine what the disordered attachments in our lives might be. Furthermore, it takes more than just noticing them to continue along the path of becoming free of them. We also need to act. We need to choose. We need to name and confront and reject that which leads to destruction and isolation, and to choose and invite in that which brings life, that which is relationship.

When we let the person of Jesus into our lives, when we let the Holy Spirit guide us, and when we let the Father call us his beloved son or beloved daughter, then you and I become our true selves. We discover who we really are.

The enemy is good at tricking us into cultivating beliefs about ourselves that are false. The false self is one who, for one reason or another, is stuck in isolation. This isolation of the false self might be the result of looking down on others or the opposite: laboring under the sense that everyone else is rightly looking down on me. Either way, when I fall into the isolation of the false self, I become paralyzed. The enemy wins.

I need to fight back. Fighting back on my own, by my own efforts, is a lost cause. Fighting back by letting the love of the Father, the friendship of Jesus, and the peace of the Holy Spirit take over, is a sure thing.

Engaging in the Battle

It is intriguing that Ignatius calls the devil "the enemy." More precisely, he calls him the enemy of our human nature. The enemy is the one who tries to distort who we are truly made to be: we are made for relationship, for friendship, for speaking, and for listening. We are made for love—both giving and receiving it. Anything that interrupts or hinders love is to be rejected. This is where we need to do battle.

Doing battle with the devil sounds daunting, to say the least. I don't feel up to it, and you probably don't either. But it's important to note here that the Christian belief is not that the devil is some kind of "bad god." He's not nearly as powerful as God. He is nowhere in the same ballpark. There is only one God. And the devil, or the enemy, has no chance against God. He gets good at tricking us to turn in on ourselves and away from God, but he has no power whatsoever against God. That's why we have to call on God, to draw close to the Heart of Christ, in our spiritual battles. When we remember to do this, we discover—to our great joy and to the up building of our confidence—that the enemy is, as Ignatius would say, a coward.

Three Images for the Enemy

There are different ways in which the enemy manifests his cowardice, but three metaphors that Ignatius uses shed light on this cowardice. (Remember that all metaphors have limitations and shouldn't be taken too literally. Yet they can help us remember how the enemy operates.)

Persona 1: The Nagging Woman

In his Rules for Discernment of Spirits, Ignatius compares the enemy to a nagging woman who, confronted with firmness and confidence, cowers.

If we can get past the political incorrectness of this image here, we can appreciate the comparison. The enemy badgers, demeans, and beats us down. In the book of Revelation, the enemy is referred to as the accuser. This is what Ignatius is getting at.

We can get accustomed to hearing the voice of discouragement. It becomes so familiar that it is part of the background noise of our lives, of our ordinary awareness.

You're gonna blow this. You can't do it. You used to be good and capable but not anymore. There are a million younger, smarter people who can do this job better than you.

Look how competent/popular/attractive _____ is. Why can't you be more like that?

There's no way you're going to be able to control yourself that long. Sure, you've promised to wait, and you're doing okay in the chastity department so far, but who are you kidding? You'll never be able to persevere. Just give in, as does everyone else.

Nagging, nagging, nagging. And the more we listen, the more run down and defeated we get. As long as we listen to this discouragement and don't step up, speak up, and confront that voice, we become paralyzed in shame, powerlessness, discouragement, and self-loathing.

Persona 2: The Licentious Man

Ignatius's second image of the enemy is a licentious man. This sleazy guy creeps around, seducing women into illicit affairs. And once he's got them in a place of shame, he won't let them out of his grip. "You ought to be ashamed of yourself. Look what you've done! You're a loser, a fraud, worthless. You'll be ruined if anyone finds out! You must keep it a secret!"

The *it* that must not be brought out into light can vary. It can be anything, really. But the effect is the same. The enemy gets us trapped and feeling as if we can never let out into the light what has gone wrong, what we're sorry for, and what we need forgiveness for. Despite our sorrow at what we have done, the enemy seeks to prevent us from availing ourselves of the only thing that can cure us: acknowledging the truth.

A Movie Metaphor: King Théoden. In order to strip away the false self and experience the freedom God wants us to have, we must find the courage to face the truth about ourselves. We find a dramatic example of this in the second of the *Lord of the Rings* movies, *The Two Towers.* The good guys are trying to join forces against the bad guys and, as in any epic struggle, the good guys look as if they don't stand a chance. They are small, underfunded, and disorganized. (Sounds like the Church, right?)

In one of the movie's most memorable scenes, the good wizard Gandalf, who has recently gone through a kind of resurrection (getting the picture?), comes with a few of his ragtag crew to recruit the once great and honorable King Théoden to help in the cause. In the old days, he had ruled well and courageously; now the great king is sitting on his throne, slumped over and drooling, looking as if he's about eight hundred years old. He is wrinkled, weak, and decrepit and can barely speak.

At the king's side is a sleazy character aptly named Wormtongue, the king's primary consultant. Over the years, the clever, deceitful Wormtongue has had the king's ear and, with his constant words of discouragement, has succeeded in coaxing the king into giving up in the struggle against evil. The king has come to believe that he is indeed powerless against the forces of evil that surround his little kingdom.

Into this throne room sneak Gandalf and his posse. They are about to make a direct plea to the once noble and powerful king to join the forces of good for a definitive stand against the enemy. But when Wormtongue sees what's going on, he goes on defense. He must keep the king from hearing anything but the lies he has been telling him. Wormtongue screams for the guards, trying to banish these truth tellers from the palace.

In all the commotion, Gandalf casts off his gray cloak to reveal his true glorified self. Gleaming in radiant white, he pounds his staff on the tile floor, points directly at Wormtongue, and bellows, "Silence!" And the enemy falls silent. Wormtongue scurries away like a coward—an enraged coward but a coward nonetheless. Free of the enemy, King Théoden is for the most part restored to his true self. And from there he enters into the mission of the one who brought him freedom and who has beaten back the enemy by direct confrontation: "Silence!"

Whether the enemy acts as a nagging woman or as a licentious man, he is defeated, as is Wormtongue, by exposure. Exposed, the enemy withers. When his deceits are confronted head-on and brought into the light, he flees like a coward. In the presence of light and truth, the enemy acts as does a cockroach that scurries away when the lights get flicked on in the kitchen. (I'm thinking of my college apartment.)

How often has a secret, shame, or fear in your life seemed like a huge deal but, when it finally came out into the light, you were amazed at how relatively small the whole issue was? This is often our experience in confession. People sometimes stay away from this sacrament for years and much of a lifetime because they have been convinced by the enemy that they are no good and that God certainly doesn't want anything to do with them. They also often project resentment onto the Church for these feelings of shame, as if the Church has created their deep guilt and shame.

As a pastor, I often heard people in the community joke but in a serious way, "I can't come to Church. The roof would cave in!" That line has become a cliché because it is such a common sentiment. People joke about it, but underneath, there is a real sense of unworthiness in the hearts of many people—maybe most people. If people would speak their shame to the Heart of Christ in the confessional, Christ could forgive and banish all discouragement the way he wants to. People could be welcomed back into communion, into relationship. And yet so many stay away, stay in isolation. They listen to that nagging and manipulative voice of the enemy saying to them, "Your past is too

ugly. You don't belong in Church. If you come out into the light,
everyone will realize what a hypocrite you are. Stay in the shad-
ows where you belong!" The only way to overcome that fear
and darkness is to bring it into the light. Speak the truth. That
truth is light, and when it is spoken, as Jesus says, it sets us free
(See Jn 8:32).

Persona 3: The Enemy Commander

Ignatius's third image of the enemy is a military commander. As
a commander circles and reconnoiters the perimeter of a fortress
that he intends to invade, the enemy of our human nature seeks
to find the vulnerable point of entry into our own hearts and
souls. When he finds that weak point—and he always does—he
exploits it immediately and continually. The manner of approach
might change, depending upon the circumstances, but the basic
pattern of exploiting that weak point in the fortress does not
change.

By recalling our core wounds, discovered in prayer and
especially through the Examen, we can better understand
exactly where those weak points might be in our own hearts,
our own souls, and our own unique histories. Although healing
is possible, it is likely that this core wound will remain a weak
spot of vulnerability, the primary place of spiritual battle. The
enemy will continue to try to exploit it, even after periods of real
healing have occurred.

Even so, we do not have to give in and accept defeat. The
gift of the redeeming love that comes from the pierced Heart of
Christ is also always offered uniquely for you and for me, healing that core wound in our hearts. When we continue to invite

the Lord into that weak spot, not only do we defeat the enemy but also, more important, we become holy. Yes, becoming holy means we are recognizing where we most need the Lord and where we can no longer take care of things ourselves.

St. Paul said that he can no longer boast in himself but only in his weakness. "I will rather boast most gladly of my weaknesses, in order that the power of Christ may dwell with me. Therefore, I am content with weaknesses, insults, hardships, persecutions, and constraints, for the sake of Christ; for when I am weak, then I am strong" (2 Cor 12:9–10).

Like St. Paul, we can become stronger than ever, not by our own efforts but only by the love of Christ working within us.

Another Movie Metaphor: Jaguar Paw in Apocalypto. This final image of the enemy acting like the military commander seeking the weak spot in the fortress is memorably captured in a scene from the movie *Apocalypto*. The story is set several centuries ago in what is now Guatemala. Again, we've got good guys and bad guys, and as always, the good ones are smaller and weaker than the bad ones. In this case, there are two Indian tribes in battle against each other. The smaller, peaceful tribe is just trying to survive, on the brink of extinction. The larger, hostile tribe is seeking to wipe out the little guys.

For quite a while the good ones intelligently defend themselves by avoiding attack from the hostile tribe. One day, though, that defense breaks down, and the bad guys swoop down on the good guys' village and begin to wreak havoc. Carnage and chaos ensue.

In the course of the action, the chief of the good guys, Flint Sky, is captured, along with his son, Jaguar Paw. While the battle swirls around them, the son apologizes to his father for failing to protect the village. As the father and son plan their escape, the lead warrior of the bad guys recognizes that he has in his captivity the little tribe's chief and his son. Seizing the opportunity, he confronts Flint Sky, lifts him up, slits his throat, and drops him in the dirt. The enemy then looks over to the son, and says, "You almost saved your father. From now on your name is *Almost*."

This is how the enemy operates. He preys upon our experience of weakness or vulnerability and then imposes a false identity, gives us a false name based on that painful experience. He says, "This is who you are." Not only do difficult, painful things *happen to us* but the enemy also wants us to believe that those experiences, those weaknesses, comprise our very identity. Above all, he wants us to forget, deny, or outright reject who we truly are: beloved sons and daughters of the Father.

But this is not the end of the story. Jaguar Paw, burdened with shame and guilt, manages to escape from the bad guys. Once he breaks free, he runs for his life as his many pursuers try to kill him. As the chase continues through the jungle, the young man comes to the top of a huge waterfall. He springs over the cliff and plunges into the waters that will surely bring his death (sound familiar, that plunging into waters as a sign of death?).

But, of course, Jaguar Paw doesn't die. His head pops up out of the water, and he scrambles to the bank of the river. He looks up and sees the infuriated enemy above, staring down at him from the top of the waterfall. Looking up at his captor, the young man catches his breath, stands up straight, and screams out to the enemy, "I am Jaguar Paw, son of Flint Sky. My father hunted this forest before me. My name is Jaguar Paw. I am a hunter. This is my forest. And my sons will hunt it with their sons when I am gone!"

After plunging into those waters, the young warrior's false self dies, and his true self is restored. He knows that he has a future. He can act. He knows who he is in part because he knows to whom he belongs. He is not Almost; he is Jaguar Paw, the son of Flint Sky.

When the enemy attacks our vulnerable point, he must be confronted head on and renounced. He tells us a big lie about ourselves, to isolate and shame us. We need to reject that lie, die to that false self, and hear the truth in that very same weak spot. We must remember who we truly are. We must remember our true name and to whom we belong. We must be confirmed in that identity.

"You are my beloved son. In you I am well pleased."

"You are my beloved daughter."

"You are my espoused."

"You are my delight."

"You are the apple of my eye."

These are the names the Father gives to us in the scripture. These are the names we have to remember.

Retreat with the Lord

Have you identified your core wounds, your greatest areas of vulnerability? Praying the Examen each day helps us to recognize these things and can lead us to much greater freedom and joy. If you are having trouble identifying your areas of weakness, or if you would like to experience deeper healing, you might consider making a retreat. A few days in silence, asking the help of the Holy Spirit, and with the assistance of a good spiritual director, can be a wonderful way to discover and strengthen your areas of great vulnerability.

In silence, we become more acutely aware of our sins, our distorted attitudes. Soon, if we keep asking what's underneath all this, it will become clear what woundedness lies beneath all this mess in our hearts. And then we can let Jesus in, let him see that vulnerable area of our hearts; he will indeed come close and love us there.

Jesus heals but not in a magical way. It is healing to be loved even after we reveal an ugly side of ourselves. If the loved one isn't repelled by that ugly part of us but reassures us of wanting to come even closer so we don't feel alone in that area, that's healing. And when Jesus does this, the healing is most effective. All it takes from us is simply revealing that weak spot of our hearts, that vulnerable or fragile moment from our histories. "Come *right here*, Jesus. I don't know what to do with this. I don't know how to handle it. I can't heal myself. Come close and love me there. And then I will be healed, by your very presence close to my wounded heart."

Again, this is where memory and the heart become so essential in the spiritual life. I have to remember vividly—to see, feel, hear, taste, and smell my early experience of suffering. I have to let it come to me in the present for it is not simply something in the past. Its effects are with me now. And bringing that memory to the surface now gives Jesus access and permission to come close and to heal that wound, to redeem that part of my history and set me free in the present.

Sometimes on retreat, I'll lead someone who has recognized some painful part of his or her history in a special "remembering" exercise. I have that person sit on a couch and imagine Jesus sitting on one side and Mary on the other. Then I ask that person to imagine holding open a photo album on his or her lap, flipping from one page to the next, with several snapshots on each page. This exercise can be an effective way to invite Mary and Jesus into our memories, even our most painful ones.

Sometimes it can be easier to start with Mary. Letting our guard down with a woman, with our mom, is sometimes easier. Then we can turn to Jesus and let him in on these things as well. Just remember—together.

It's crucial to remember what is painful with another person and to bring those memories into relationship. The reason those painful memories inflict such ongoing pain and dysfunction is that we keep brooding over them, analyzing them in isolation. We get a skewed sense of our past, our history, ourselves, and our identities. We also get a skewed view of what God *probably* thinks of us in light of these memories. When we keep these memories packed away in the back of our heads, we fail to see who God really is and who we really are.

Healing through the Sacred Heart

The Sacred Heart plays an important role in our healing and becoming our authentic selves. We have already considered the nature of Jesus' heart that is pierced and yet on fire. His heart is wounded by the world and yet remains open and on fire with love. Now what about our hearts?

When considering surfacing these wounded areas of our past through prayer, we are imitating Jesus in opening our hearts again even though they too have been pierced. And when our hearts are open again, we are brought into relationship. Our hearts can once again be set on fire. We will discover that we have a greater capacity to love and to hope than we thought we had before. Some parts of our hearts feel as if they died a long time ago. But in this way of praying, we are given hearts back that are alive and new—still wounded but more ready to love than ever. In fact, maybe we are now able to love, to be more sympathetic and compassionate than ever, *because* we have gone through this process of recognizing our wounds and given them to Jesus for healing.

When we go to the doctor, we don't just tell him, "I don't feel well." If we did, the doctor might respond, "Is this not feeling well going on in the top half or the bottom half of you? Can you be more specific? Where does it hurt?" It helps to be as precise as we can in pointing out the hurts in our own hearts as well. And it helps to have the language that can do justice to what's going on.

An Invitation

In this second portion of the book, we have tried to explore the important role that the Examen or evening review can play in your daily spiritual life. In using the gift of memory, we can recall where there is life and where there is death. We can better have a sense of where the wounds are in our hearts that give way to pain and various forms of sin, selfishness, resentment, jealousy, failures in chastity, self-pity, and so on. When we become aware of these areas, we know two things: First, these are the areas that the enemy wants to exploit. Second, the Holy Spirit wants to lead Jesus to these vulnerable areas, so that he can heal and redeem us where we most need him.

On a daily basis, then, if we can hang in there with the Examen, we can make great progress in gaining more freedom and joy in our lives. Our hearts can get bigger. And then when we start the next day with the Morning Offering, we will have a better sense of what parts of our hearts we want to let go of and unite with Jesus so that we can love others with a full and free heart.

Much of this healing, progress, and redemption can be prepared by way of our personal prayer in the Morning Offering and the Examen. But to remain only in private prayer, even if we are talking heart to heart with Jesus, we will still fall short of genuine renewal of our lives and hearts. Ultimately, we want not only to speak to Jesus about where our hearts are but also to receive new hearts. We want to be able to receive his Heart as our own. This is accomplished most perfectly by going to Mass. In the celebration of the Mass, we receive Jesus' own Heart, his actual Heart, in the Eucharist. And we are receiving his Heart along with other people who are in the same boat. When we enter into communion with the Lord, we enter in communion with his whole Body, in heaven and on earth.

In the final portion of this book we turn to explore this mystery, the culmination of the Christian life that is the celebration of the Eucharist. This third moment of prayer unites and reconciles everything that the first two moments have been about: the ideals expressed in the Morning Offering and the memories recalled in the Examen all come to fruition as our hearts are sacramentally and therefore truly united to Christ's own Heart as he offers it to us in the Mass. So let's go there!

Litany of Humility
Cardinal Rafael Merry del Val

O Jesus! meek and humble of heart, Hear me.
From the desire of being esteemed,
Deliver me, Jesus.

From the desire of being loved . . .
From the desire of being extolled . . .
From the desire of being honored . . .
From the desire of being praised . . .
From the desire of being preferred to others . . .
From the desire of being consulted . . .
From the desire of being approved . . .
From the fear of being humiliated . . .
From the fear of being despised . . .
From the fear of suffering rebukes . . .
From the fear of being calumniated . . .
From the fear of being forgotten . . .
From the fear of being ridiculed . . .
From the fear of being wronged . . .
From the fear of being suspected . . .
That others may be loved more than I,
Jesus, grant me the grace to desire it.

That others may be esteemed more than I . . .
That, in the opinion of the world,
others may increase and I may decrease . . .
That others may be chosen and I set aside . . .
That others may be praised and I unnoticed . . .
That others may be preferred to me in everything . . .
That others may become holier than I,
provided that I may become as holy as I should . . .

Questions and Reflections

1. When do you feel like your "true self"? What are you doing? Who is with you? What's the context?

2. When are you given the grace of being "self-forgetful"? What is it like to not even be aware of yourself, but just totally engaged in a conversation, an activity, a task, or a relationship—in *love*?

3. When are you anxious and turned in on yourself? What is the context when you are most worried about how others are perceiving you?

4. What are your greatest areas of weakness that the enemy tries to exploit? What is the healing truth that the Father is trying to speak to your heart?

PART III

Living the Eucharist

• • •

An Exercise

If possible, go to Mass today.

Pay close attention to the prayers spoken and movements made, especially of the offertory, when the bread and wine are carried up the aisle from the people in the congregation.

Listen carefully to the consecration, when the priest speaks the word of Jesus: "This is my body . . . this is my blood."

During the fraction rite, where the bread is broken in order to be given away, and Communion itself, when the people come forward to receive Jesus, contemplate the wonder of this mystery: once again, Jesus comes among us to give us his very Self.

Meditate on how you can live your day more deliberately according to this pattern. How can you let your own heart, united with the Sacred Heart of Jesus, be blessed, broken, and given away freely in daily life? Ask for that grace.

The Offertory

• • •

Jesus said to them, "There is no need for them to
go away; give them some food yourselves." But
they said to him, "Five loaves and two fish are all
we have here." Then he said, "Bring them here to
me," and he ordered the crowds to sit down on
the grass. Taking the five loaves and the two fish,
and looking up to heaven, he said the blessing,
broke the loaves, and gave them to the disciples,
who in turn gave them to the crowds.

—Matthew 14:16–19

The Dead Sea is dead. Nothing lives in there. Why? There's
nowhere for the water to go. No tributaries flow out of there.
When there's nowhere for the stuff of life to go, the place of life
becomes death.

The same thing is true of our hearts. If there's no one around
to love, our hearts begin to dry up and die. We are made to give
our lives and our hearts away. Only when we do this can we
live. So how do we learn how to do this? Where do we get the
courage and the willingness to say yes to this plan of life?

In these next three chapters, I'd like to suggest a way of
looking at the Mass, to see that what happens in the Mass is the
perfect pattern for our daily lives. I will start with the dynamics of the offertory, move into the consecration and sacrifice at
the center of the Eucharist, and end with the act of receiving

Communion and being missioned at the end of Mass. I hope to offer something encouraging both for people who go to Mass regularly and for those who never or rarely go. Regardless of your regular practice, I hope this vision will be an occasion to see what's going on in this celebration with new eyes.

Living the Eucharist—In and Out of Church

If we pay attention to the little things that go into making the celebration of the Mass what it is, we can begin to see a pattern emerge of what life that is truly and fully lived looks like. When we let ourselves be deeply shaped by the dynamics of what happens in the Mass, then we become better equipped to staying open to the world and letting flow out from our hearts what has flowed into them. In that way, we avoid letting our hearts become miniature Dead Seas! "Living a eucharistic life" becomes all that it means to be truly human.

In the previous chapters, I've suggested the image of the pierced and enflamed Heart of Jesus as a model for what our hearts should be. We've seen how to share our lives and enter deeply into the Heart of Christ through the Morning Offering. We've explored how to become who we really can be by refusing to stay in the isolation of our false selves and by submitting our weaknesses to the healing power of the Lord through the Examen, and how these two prayers of the heart are like "bookends" of daily living.

Now we're going to look at what happens between those two moments: how to live with a heart that is opened in love to the world, even if it means getting dinged up, and trusting that when our hearts do get pierced along the way, they will not get done in. They can remain on fire with love.

The God Who Breaks Through to Us

It is a key to the vision of the Apostleship of Prayer that the Eucharist is a "mystery to be believed, celebrated, and then lived." This is a basic teaching of the Church. In the Second Vatican Council, the Church taught that the celebration of the Eucharist is the "source and summit of the Christian life" (*Lumen Gentium* 11). It's where we get our life, the most perfect thing we do every day. Or better, it can be the most perfect act we can *participate in* every day. There's something perfect about the dynamics of the liturgy of the Eucharist, the actions into which we are drawn that get us where we most need to be.

What is so perfect about the action of the Mass? It starts with the fact that the Mass is primarily not something we do to try to get to God. Rather, the Mass is God's perfect attempt to get to us, to get into our hearts, in order to bring us to life and ultimately to bring us home to live forever with his own Heart.

In her book *The Essence of Prayer*, Ruth Burrows, a Carmelite sister, has noted how different Christian prayer is. In the Christian reality, even though we sometimes forget it, it is not up to us to reach up to God, to do something special to get God's attention, so that he will listen to us. God has already come down to us and broken through "the veil" that existed between us. We don't have to go up the mountain to find God. In fact, we couldn't do it if we wanted to. We just don't have what it takes.

But God knows that. That's why he comes down to us. He comes down from the heights and makes himself small, a defenseless baby in the womb of a young girl in Nazareth, to be born helpless and poor. God, who is great, has become small in Jesus. God, who is infinite, became finite, limited, just like us, in the person of Jesus. It's for this reason that we can pray—not from our strength and discipline but precisely from where we feel weak, where we feel small and powerless. In fact, this is the most important place to be praying from in our hearts.

When Jesus shows us his Heart that is vulnerable, pierced, and bloody, that's a cue for us. It's an invitation to us to say, "If you can expose your heart to me, to the world, then I can do the same to you, Lord." We have places in our hearts that hurt, that are wounded, and that seem outside the scope of what God should be concerned about. If you're like me, you usually want to pray from a place of which you're proud, where you're well behaved, serene, and upstanding. This isn't where we need God.

We need him where things are screwed up, where there is darkness and shame. We need him where we feel alone, where we feel as if we're beyond help. We need God to come into the places where we have given up on new life. And that's where he wants to go too. The celebration of the Eucharist is about letting God into these places in our lives where we need him.

Prayers of Thorns and Fire

It helps at this point to return to the central Christian image of the Sacred Heart of Jesus. When we look upon the image of the Sacred Heart, we see him pointing to his heart that is on the outside, opened up in vulnerability to us, to the world. In that exposure of his heart, his heart is pierced. His heart is wounded. But it is also on fire with life and love.

This is our hope. Jesus says to us through that image, "This is the way I live. This is the way I love. And you can, too. In fact, you must." This is the only way to live and have life to the fullest: if we expose our hearts in loving trust to the world even if it means that our hearts will be pierced. I realize that I will be wounded when I open my heart, but my heart will remain on fire if I do. The only way the fire will go out is if I refuse to keep opening up my heart in daily life.

When we are united with Christ in Baptism, and sustained in our union with him in the reception of the sacraments, especially Reconciliation and the Eucharist, we too come to have a heart, little by little, that is like the Heart of Jesus. In fact, when we receive the Eucharist, we take his Heart into our own. St. Augustine said, when it comes to every other food we take into our bodies, that food becomes us, becomes part of our bodies. But when we receive Communion, the food we receive doesn't become us but rather we become that food, the Body of Christ. Only because we are letting God into our lives like this and letting him take over our lives can we begin to live the lives we are made for, lives characterized by perfect love.

A Miraculous Exchange

At the very end of the Spiritual Exercises, St. Ignatius explains that "love expresses itself more in deeds than in words" and that love consists in giving and receiving of gifts between the lover and the beloved. Love is not just happy thoughts or good wishes about another or for another. Love takes action. It involves risking oneself and giving away the gifts one has for the good of another.

Jesus described this mystery a variety of ways but rather poignantly when he said, "Unless a grain of wheat falls to the ground and dies, it remains just a grain of wheat; but if it dies, it produces much fruit" (Jn 12:24). This sentiment is not simply something Jesus talked about. He lived it. And not only did he live it outwardly in his actions but also expressed this truth in his very identity: to be fully alive, to be one's true self, is to give oneself away.

In one of the oldest hymns of the New Testament, St. Paul describes what it means to "have the same attitude as Christ." It means to empty oneself. The Greek term *kenosis*, to empty, is at the heart of this vision. St. Paul tells the earliest followers of Jesus that Christ himself, "though he was in the form of God, did not regard equality with God something to be grasped. Rather, he emptied himself, taking the form of a slave, coming in human likeness" (Phil 2:6–7).

This way of describing the Incarnation, that central Christian mystery, points to what it means to be a human being. It also reveals what it means to be God. God himself, in all his power, knowledge, glory, and transcendence, does not cling to or grasp at this power and transcendence but rather *empties* himself of it. But as he empties himself of himself, he does not lose himself. Rather, this is the *way he is*. Emptying oneself of one's power is not a departure from what it is to be God—it *defines* what it is to be God. God is the one who gives himself away, out of love. And if this is what God is like, then we as humans, who are created in the image of God (See Gn 1:27), discover what it means to be who we are created to be in emptying ourselves out, for love. One way of describing the deep structure of the Mass is precisely in these terms, a giving and receiving of gifts between Lover and the Community of the Beloved—that's us!

The Offertory

The action of gift giving and receiving in the Mass is made concrete after what is called the Liturgy of the Word. Having listened to and responded to scriptural readings and having reflected on the Word together in the priest or deacon's homily, it's time to move from words to deeds.

The liturgy of the Eucharist begins with the offertory. Maybe the first thing worth saying here is that this doesn't look like much. I'm not just talking here about how it looks from the side of the pastor who needs to pay the bills. All those single dollar bills in the baskets must get a bit discouraging. But I'm not talking about money here. I'm talking about what's at the center of the offertory. What exactly are the gifts coming up the aisle, and how are they offered?

There might be a procession, perhaps with some nice background music. The gifts are brought forward in precious vessels—precious not only because of what they are made of but also for what transpires in them later in the Mass.

At the moment of that offering, though, what's in those vessels? Not much. Some bits of unleavened bread and a little wine. Not much for the crowd that fills the pews in the church on a Sunday; these people have come looking for something. We are looking to feed the hunger, the longing that resides in our hearts.

Entering the Dialogue

Once those gifts are sent up the aisle with that little bit of unleavened bread and wine, they are placed into the hands of the priest who stands before the people of God *in persona Christi*. And he starts speaking. Speaking "with the I of Christ," the priest begins a dialogue with God the Father.

First, he thanks the Father for the gifts that have been given and raises them in a gesture of recognition that these came from the Father's goodness in creation in the first place. It is "fruit of the earth and work of human hands."

This bread and wine, and everything else we have in our lives, are gifts from God. Once this prayer of thanksgiving is complete, the priest proclaims that these apparently meager gifts "will become for us the bread of life" and "our spiritual drink."

As you watch the priest, standing there at the altar, consider: *How am I tied into this prayer? How are the whole people of God, gathered together in the church, being drawn into this dialogue between Jesus and his Father?* At the offertory, the gifts are deliberately and physically brought forward from the congregation. There is a reason for this. We bring forward what we do have even though it doesn't seem as if it's going to do much good.

Remember the stories in the gospels of Jesus feeding the multitudes, the multiplication of the loaves and fishes? After listening to Jesus' preaching, the disciples recommend to Jesus that he let the crowds go on their way so that they can find something to eat. Jesus responds saying, why don't you feed them? Giving the disciples a chance to complain that they don't have nearly enough to feed these vast crowds, Jesus tells them, "bring what you do have." The first thing he does then is thank the Father for the few loaves and the few fish that have been given. He has no doubt that this will be enough. Only the disciples doubt the adequacy of the gifts.

The next time you're at Mass, when that offertory time comes, as you watch those gifts being brought forward to the altar by a regular family—imagine it is your own heart being sent up that aisle, your own heart placed in those vessels of precious metal.

What is your own heart like at that moment? Maybe it's feeling pretty good. Maybe it's pretty joyful, confident, and free. Maybe you've got a new girlfriend next to you, and she seems so excellent you can't believe she's going out with you. Maybe you're holding your newborn baby, and you are overwhelmed by the gift God has given you and your husband in this new little person. Maybe you have a calm steadiness in your heart. Your family is growing up well. The kids are a bit difficult here and there, but you're glad they seem to be getting along and basically doing well in their studies, perhaps finding their first jobs and generally coming into their own.

On the other hand, maybe things are not so hot. Maybe work is crushing your spirit, demanding more and more of you with no extra pay or recognition to go along with it. Maybe you're feeling like an expendable cog in a machine. Maybe you've lost your father recently and are still haunted by what you never had a chance to say to him. Maybe you miss your family who lives far away. Maybe you keep wondering if that one relationship might ever be able to be repaired or if it's lost forever.

There are lots of possibilities. What kind of heart am I sending up that aisle? Take a moment at the offertory to pay attention to what your heart is like. Ideally, you might have done that before getting to Mass. If you did get there a minute or two early to just calm down, maybe you had the chance to check in and see where your heart was this morning. What kind of an offering am I making here today at the Mass? What kind of a heart does God have to work with here? What is needed?

Seeing with New Eyes

Maybe you don't get to Mass very often. If so, this could be an especially helpful exercise. You could start to see what's going on there with new eyes. Maybe you're very clear about why you're there and what you're seeking from Jesus. But most of the time if we're at Mass, there's a good chance we haven't put a huge amount of thought and deliberation into being there.

There's nothing wrong with routine. It's better than not going at all. But from within this routine, maybe I can set myself up for an unexpected moment of wonder as I allow myself to enter into the mystery. That little bit of bread and wine that is going up the aisle is shortly going to be coming back to me as the "bread of life" and the "chalice of eternal salvation"; this Body and Blood of Christ is everything God has to give me, his very self. That's what I'm going to be receiving in a few moments. That's a big difference.

Something happens in the course of the Eucharistic Prayer. In the course of this dialogue that begins between the Son and the Father and united together by the Love that is the Holy Spirit, those meager gifts that come from the fields, from the ordinary material of creation and "the work of human hands," are in the process of becoming something we can't even begin to understand. The gifts change, big time.

What about my heart? When I let go of my heart, send it down the aisle, and let it be placed on the altar; when I first thank God for the heart and the life that I do have; and when I call down the power of the Holy Spirit upon my heart and the gift of my life, could it be that things change on my end as well? It's almost indiscernible at first. No, on second thought, it's totally indiscernible that something is happening. But take the time to let it play out. When I just let go of my life and let it get inserted into the life of God, when that life of mine comes back to me, it comes back different—really different.

What If I Refuse?

Let's look at it from the other side. What if I don't let go of my life and hand it over in this manner? If I keep my heart to myself and try to handle life on my own, things get pretty small. My heart gets puny and shrivels up. If I never risk letting go of my heart, to place it into the hands and the heart of the Lord, it remains small and rather useless, frankly. It's like that grain of wheat that never falls to the ground and gets crushed into the soil. It just lays there on the surface, self-contained and protected but ultimately lifeless and not good for much. It just shrivels up and dies.

Whatever is going on in my life, whether it's good or bad, it must be handed over into relationship. If there are bad things going on in my life, I must not be burdened with them alone. Things will get toxic. If there's sin in my life, I must speak it out to another, to Christ, and allow his mercy to take over. If I am overcome with shame in my life or feelings of inadequacy, I must offer that over, so that I can be reminded of the truth of my life. I am abundantly, unconditionally loved.

I don't know what my heart is like until it is handed over to another, and ultimately to the Lord. Only when it is shared; when I thank the Father for what has been given; and when I let Jesus receive the gifts that I do have and the Holy Spirit is called down upon them do these gifts start to become what they can be and what they are meant to be.

I have an uncle who died a couple of years ago. He had had some tough stretches in life. He had always been great fun to be around when I was growing up and was very generous with family and friends. His first marriage ended as his two children were just approaching the teenage years. He had struggled a bit with alcohol, perhaps burdened by some shame. After the divorce and the difficulties with his kids and family, he also left the Church for a time. Most of his foundational relationships were severed.

Later, he married a second time, and many years into their marriage his new wife decided she wanted to become a Catholic. My uncle wasn't too interested, but she proceeded with the program. Both of them had to get annulments from previous marriages, and finally she was ready for entrance into the life of the Catholic Church. Exactly at that time, my uncle discovered he had cancer. He soon had to quit his job because he just didn't have the physical stamina for it anymore.

It seemed that he had lost everything. But when his wife entered the Church, my uncle found his way back to the Church too. A new regular routine for him emerged. And for my dad too. The two brothers who had been rather estranged over the years started going together to daily Mass on a regular basis. They went to the VA hospital for Mass—a nice short one that suited these two brothers very well.

At the hospital they met a wonderful priest, the chaplain, who came there for various medical treatments. My uncle found himself in a new situation. Even as he felt as if he had been cut off at the knees by this cancer diagnosis, he also found himself around other people who were weakened as well, not only physically but also emotionally, both by the effects of war and because of relationships that had been strained or broken from their service to their country. Somehow, my uncle found a special sort of home there.

My uncle had lost his job and the security of good health, but after returning to the sacraments, he discovered a sense of purpose he hadn't had for many years. He made a good, solid confession to this wonderful new priest and soon became a "daily masser" at the little chapel in the VA hospital. He started bringing some old ladies in the neighborhood out grocery shopping once a week. His favorite "girlfriend" was well into her nineties and blind.

By the time my uncle died, his relationships with his family, though not perfect, had greatly improved. At the moment of his death, he was surrounded by his wife, his daughter, his grandson, his brother (my dad), and my mom. I was celebrating Mass at the foot of his bed, and as the little bit of bread and wine were being prayed over and placed on the altar, my uncle breathed his last breath.

I believe that, somewhere deep in his consciousness, in his heart, my uncle surrendered himself at that moment of the offertory. It was like the whole of his life—the good stuff, the love that he did have, and the weaknesses that he also had—all of it, was simply taken up by the Lord in that moment of the offering of the gifts of the bread and wine and turned into something glorious.

What a way to let go of this life and begin the next! It was especially beautiful to witness this, given my uncle's difficult history. All the wounds of his life here on earth were transformed once they were placed into the hands of the Lord and once he started letting the Lord into these wounds of his life. The Lord does have his way. And even what looks to us like something not worthy of association with God—maybe this is what becomes especially beautiful and holy once it is humbly handed over to God.

An Invitation

Ultimately, the Mass teaches us how to surrender and in turn to receive what we most need. We learn these things not just by taking into our own hearts the Heart of Jesus in the Eucharist but also through the dynamics that precede Communion.

Through the giving and the receiving of gifts, we are reminded of the mystery of *kenosis*, of relinquishment and renunciation of that which is precious, every time we go to Mass. Not only are we reminded of it but we are also *enacted into* that very reality. We encounter the God who *empties* himself and who lets himself be handed over to us in order to give us what we need most. And having received this love of God made flesh in the Eucharist, we return to the world outside the church doors, letting ourselves be sent out there to be handed over, emptied out, and given away for those who most need the love we now have to offer.

To the believers in Corinth, St. Paul wrote, "I handed on to you as of first importance what I also received: that Christ died for our sins in accordance with the scriptures" (1 Cor 15:3). In the Mass, what we are handed is not just the proclamation that Jesus died for us but also Christ himself, in the flesh and in the Eucharist, so that our lives can be transformed by his love that changes us, that brings us back to life from the place of sin and death. When we encounter love like this, concretely and sacramentally in the Mass, and if we let it impact our hearts, we start living a different way in our daily lives. We have the same confidence he does to surrender himself out of love so that others might live. And in so doing, we come to live the lives we are made for and thus experience the fullness of life and genuine freedom.

The Suscipe
St. Ignatius of Loyola

Take, Lord, and receive all my liberty,
my memory, my understanding,
and my entire will,
All I have and call my own.
You have given all to me.
To you, Lord, I return it.
Everything is yours; do with it what you will.
Give me only your love and your grace,
that is enough for me.

Questions and Reflections

1. What do you *wish* you had to offer to God, to the world, to your family, to your community, and so forth?

2. What do you *actually* have to offer to them?

3. How will you offer that today?

The Sacrifice

· · ·

And I will pour out . . . a spirit of compassion
and supplication, so that, when they look on him
whom they have pierced, they shall mourn for
him. . . .

—Zechariah 12:10, RSV

Right after I was ordained a priest, I spent the first two years
as a pastor on the Pine Ridge Indian Reservation. In the
culture of the Oglala Lakota people, great importance is placed
on the reality of death and the mystery of eternal life. When a
person is sick and close to dying, it is not uncommon for many
members of the family to drop everything, go to the hospital
two hours away in Rapid City, and spend hours upon hours,
days upon days, there with their dying loved one. When the
person finally dies, the wake is planned: two nights of visitation
to honor the deceased, with many stories and shared laughter
and tears.

The night before the funeral and burial, the family often asks
that a rosary be said and a Mass be offered—even though many
of them are not practicing Catholics. Even so, it had become the
custom for pastors to choose five mysteries from all the mysteries of the rosary—the joyful, luminous, sorrowful, and glorious—in order to recount for the benefit of all those at the wake
the story of Jesus' life, death, and resurrection.

The custom also provided an opportunity for all those gathered together to see the life of the one who had died as having lived and died within that story of Jesus. No matter who the person was and no matter what could be said about that person's life and character, somehow the most important aspects, the truest moments of the person's life, could be found within the story of Jesus. Anything that was true and good and beautiful from a person's experience in life could be seen in the light of Jesus' life.

There is only one story. Every human life takes part within the life of Christ. To make sense of our own lives on a day-to-day basis, we do well to come back to that one story again and again. We find our true selves within that story. Specifically, within the moment of prayer that is the celebration of the Eucharist, we find our true selves in the concentrated narrative of Jesus. In living the Eucharist, we offer ourselves just as the Lord offered himself in love out of obedience to his Father, for the sake of the salvation of the world, including those who betrayed him and plotted his death. This is the story that culminates in the sacrifice of the Mass, when Jesus offers to us his whole self, his very Body and Blood, "for the forgiveness of sins" so that we might live.

Surrendering Myself to the Story

If the eucharistic liturgy is the culminating moment of our day, this means that each movement within the liturgy enacts what is essential for our lives, even in our more ordinary circumstances. In the last chapter, we considered the fruitfulness of offering our gifts, our hearts, and our lives to the life of the Trinity, just as we do in the offertory at Mass. What happens once we begin that surrender?

In the act of surrendering, we recognize that we are not in control. But that's not a desperate realization. It's a comforting one, a consoling one. It's a good thing I'm not in control of life! Someone else is in control, someone who can do a better job with it. That someone is God, who has become human and who acts for us the way we'd like to act and the way we'd like to live. Our gesture of communal surrender at the offertory in the Mass is an invitation for Christ to take over, to start speaking and to start loving *for* us, so that we can truly live.

After the offertory gesture and prayers comes the longer Eucharistic Prayer; at the heart of this prayer is the consecration, or the "institution narrative." It's telling the story of the Last Supper. "When he was at table with those he loved . . . " The priest begins by recalling what happened "back when," when Jesus was speaking to his disciples. Then, suddenly the past becomes present as Christ speaks his own words through the priest at the altar, so that we who are gathered together can hear the direct communication from Christ. We in the congregation are drawn into a direct conversation with Jesus.

"Take this all of you and eat it. This is my body, which will be given up for you.

"Take this all of you and drink from it. This is the chalice of my blood, the blood of the new and eternal covenant. It will be poured out for you and for many for the forgiveness of sins."

Then he gives a command that pertains to the future: "Do this in memory of me." And in celebrating the Mass, in that moment we are staying true to the promise that he asked his disciples to keep and which he continues to ask us to keep today. It is in this celebration of the Eucharist, then, that the perfect conversation takes place. And when we enter into it, we remember who we truly are, where we belong, and where we're going.

Somehow in the process of telling and listening to the story of what happened two thousand years ago, on the night before Jesus was killed, the Church bears witness all over the world, in every place and time, that this is not merely a historical account. Through the liturgy, we are drawn into our own dialogue with Jesus himself. He speaks in the first person: this is my body. And he speaks to us in the second person: "Take this, all of you. . . . My body will be given up for you."

Saying and Doing

In the dialogue of the liturgy, the dialogue between Christ and us is perfectly accomplished. In our daily lives, the flow of this dialogue is not as neat and easy. In fact, we often drop out of the dialogue. (I know I do.) Paying attention to what is being said in this moment of the consecration sheds light on how our lives can and must unfold in order for this dialogue to be restored.

In the liturgy, we experience the Eucharistic Prayer not just in words of the priest but in his actions as well: kissing the altar, washing the hands, elevating the elements, bowing, genuflecting, and so forth. Each of these movements directs our attention to the central action of the Eucharist taking place on the altar: the sacrifice of Christ. Jesus' words at the Last Supper on Holy Thursday anticipated what would happen on Good Friday. He announced that he would give up his body and blood the next day on the Cross.

As those words are spoken in the Mass, they do not anticipate the future but reenact something in the present. The sacrifice of Jesus on the Cross is re-presented; the one and only sacrifice he made on the Cross two thousand years ago is manifest here and now, today. Jesus promised to love us to the end on

Holy Thursday at the Last Supper. He did it again on the Cross. And now, every time the Mass is celebrated, he becomes present in the Eucharist, giving us everything he's got. His presence is broken open and poured out for us, so that we might receive it all.

I recently took part in a conversation on Relevant Radio, talking about Palm Sunday and the significance of the Passion in anticipation of Holy Week. We acknowledged that sometimes in our culture, even in the lives of devout people, the story of the Passion of Jesus can lose the power to move us. We become accustomed to hearing it over and over in our lives. Then a woman called in and described how her husband, a veteran, has been in and out of the VA hospital with a whole slew of problems. The doctors couldn't do much to help him, and they often feel confused and helpless. But then she testified that when she goes to the hospital for the various procedures her husband is having, she goes to the chapel and sits and looks at the crucifix. She speaks to Christ in the Blessed Sacrament in the tabernacle and thanks him for the way that he joined himself to her suffering and her husband's suffering. As she described this situation and the kind of prayer (dialogue with Jesus) that she undertakes, she began to weep. So did I, and probably many listeners around the country joined us in those tears.

In one brief moment, by telling the story of her own passion and the passion of her husband at this moment, she led us all back into the one story of Jesus. She led us back to the Cross and not just the story of the Cross from a long time ago but also the person of Jesus right now who is alive and well and with us in the Eucharist. She showed us how to speak to him. She showed us how to listen to Jesus who spoke to us from the Cross. What he spoke there was that he is with us in our suffering and even our death. He spoke that to his disciples the night before at the Last Supper. He speaks it to us every day in the celebration of the Eucharist. "This is my body which will be given up for you."

The Power of Remembering

When the same old stories get told in new settings, under different circumstances, at different times of life, we actually hear them in new ways. They become not just the same old stories but also stories that form us and shape our self-understanding in new ways. In a sense, we are made new in the hearing of them. As a result, we are given new confidence to live with more clarity and purpose when we go back to ordinary life.

This is just a glimpse of the much deeper reality of what goes on in the Mass. In the very short consecration narrative, we are given in a few words the vision of who God is and who we are in relationship to God. Christ himself, who is both God and man, shows us at one time both who God is and who we are made to be. He shows us how we can be our true selves only in relationship to God and only by radically trusting in God's care when everything else around us is falling apart—trusting even when things fail, when we experience suffering and even death. In the sacrifice of Christ on the Cross, we see that hope makes sense. It works even in the face of what looks like defeat and death. This is our story.

Just before the consecration is a short prayer, the "preface," which changes depending on the feast day or the liturgical season of the year. And yet they also have a unifying theme: they anticipate what is about to happen in the consecration, the turning point of salvation history. And after the consecration comes what is called the anamnesis, the remembering. Having just been drawn into the sacrifice of Christ in the consecration, the people, through the priest, speak to the Father and ask him to remember us in the Church: the pope, our bishop, the faithful throughout the world, and especially those who have died who are on their way into eternal life with the Trinity by the help of our own prayers at that moment. And as we ask the Father to remember us and the covenant he has extended to us, we ourselves remember even more deeply who we are and what is in store for us in heaven.

And the Reality of Forgetfulness

This is pretty beautiful stuff. So why is it so hard for us to keep this vision of the Mass alive? We come back to the reality of forgetting. We forget who we are.

It was the same with Adam and Eve, tricked into forgetting the God who walked with them at the "breezy time of day." Forgetting that God had given them everything freely and lovingly, they were tricked into thinking he was holding back on his goodness and decided to take control of their lives, rather than receiving what is good with humility and gratitude.

When they realized what they had done, they became scared and ashamed, covering themselves up with the fig leaves, hiding from God who created and loved them. "Where are you?" God called to them. It's a good question for us too. When we forget who we are and where we belong, when we live in fear and hide ourselves, just trying to get by on our own, we need to remember the God who loves us too.

Some of the most moving encounters in the gospels are about people who come to Jesus in a state of confusion, and he leads them out of it by reminding them of their story. They came to Jesus asking him all kinds of questions, about divorce, marriage, and resurrection, one even devising an elaborate scenario where a woman marries seven successive men and each of them dies. Now comes the gotcha moment: in heaven, whose wife will she be?

Rather than getting drawn into the confusion, the complexity, and the divisiveness of both the question and the spirit behind the question, Jesus replies, "From the beginning it was not so" (Mt 19:8). He points them back to the original story of humanity and the way Adam and Eve are made for each other and complement each other to make possible the fullness of human life—together, in mutual self-sacrificing love. That's the real story of the human condition.

The Woman at the Well

In the fourth chapter of the Gospel of John, the woman at the well has no ulterior motives in her encounter with Jesus. She's just trying to get through the day. But she is stuck in a state of isolation from the community because of her sin, doing the wash alone at the hottest time of the day, for a reason. The other women in the community would have been doing their work early in the morning, visiting with each other—in relationship—while they worked.

Jesus sees this woman is alone and starts the conversation by showing his own need. "Give me a drink," he says. After the lengthy and elusive dialogue that ensues, the tables are turned. Jesus offers her living water that will truly satisfy her thirst, the refreshment of the Father's mercy that will deliver her from her state of sin, shame, and isolation.

But to get to the point where it's clear what she wants, and to experience the excitement that something new can happen in her life, she had to get to the point of being honest with herself, before the Lord, about what the disfigured story of her own life had been. She had to tell that story, as it were, in order to hear the deeper story of God's merciful pursuit of his beloved who had strayed away in sin.

Emmaus Road

At times we become trapped in isolation that comes, not from personal sin, but out of grief or pain. As we explore this moment of prayer that is the celebration of the Eucharist, the story of Emmaus speaks clearly to the necessity of having our eyes opened so we might respond to the love being offered to us. And once again, the first step is to be reminded of the story of which we are a part.

The disciples, who had been accompanying Jesus during his triumphant entry into Jerusalem on Palm Sunday, had also apparently been on hand to watch everything fall apart. The one in whom they had placed their confidence had been arrested, humiliated, and soundly defeated on the Cross, and though they had heard stories that he might be alive, they were heading back home to Emmaus, presumably to resume the lives they had been leading before they met Jesus. Only now their hearts were hardened by disappointment, disillusionment, and even bitterness and cynicism.

It is into this state of being downcast and turned in on themselves that Jesus comes to these disciples. He enters right into their disappointment and heartbreak. And how does he enter? He enters by asking them to tell him the story of what has been happening. Jesus wants the disciples to speak, to tell the story as best they can from their vantage point. He wants us to do the same. "Tell me what you see. How does the story go from your point of view?"

This is a great prayer to enter into daily with Jesus. No need to figure things out, to come up with a strategy for success. "Just tell me what happened." It reminds me of what happens when a kid falls off a bike or gets in a fight with a sibling or a neighbor. He runs home to Mom, and the mother takes her son into her arms and says, "Tell me what happened." She might know full well what happened, but she knows instinctively that it's good for the child to tell the story.

Well, when the two disciples on the road tell Jesus the story, they get all the facts right, but it turns out they're way off in their interpretation of the events. They take the facts of the story to mean they might as well throw in the towel and go back to life as usual. Jesus listens to the story they tell and then situates it in the larger story of salvation history. As they continue to walk along, Jesus reminds them of what God has been doing throughout all of history up to this moment. He reminds them that God had promised to save his people. A messiah would come who would suffer, but that "suffering servant" would redeem the people of God precisely by way of the suffering.

But the story doesn't really become clear until they sit down at a table to share a meal. And not until the breaking of the bread do the disciples see the whole truth. Now they know that they have not been defeated; they do not have any reason for discouragement and self-pity. Rather they have a reason to head right back to Jerusalem and start proclaiming the good news that Jesus is alive. And if he's alive now, that means that God is with them just as he has always been, even having gone through defeat with them all the way to death. Even now, on the other side of death, the victory of God, love, hope, and faith is evident. This is how the real story goes.

What is it that made the disciples see the truth? The evangelist Luke makes it clear that it was in the breaking of the bread that the disciples were able to finally see Jesus for who he was—their Lord who was killed and yet now is alive (see Lk 24:13–31). There was something about that breaking.

In John's gospel, Jesus appears again to the apostles in the Upper Room, this time with Thomas present (see John 20:24–29). Thomas refused to believe the disciples who had reported seeing the risen Lord. Thomas would have none of it. He had been so hurt by the loss of Jesus that he had hardened his heart to protect himself from being hurt again. But what is it that moves him to believe again? The wounds. When Jesus shows Thomas his wounds, Jesus was sharing the wounds that Thomas has in his own heart. Only by encountering these wounds does Thomas open his heart and believe and worship.

An Invitation

Both of these stories—the breaking of the bread at Emmaus and the wounded side in the Upper Room—signify the same reality that is presented to us in the Eucharist. In the consecration and sacrifice of the Eucharist, we experience the healing sacrifice of Jesus, just as the disciples encountered it on the way to Emmaus and Thomas in the Upper Room. What Jesus opened up in the Last Supper and on the Cross, even though it happened in the past, becomes a reality today.

His becoming present and drawing us into the healing and redemption of our hearts "in his wounds" happen every day at

Mass, most perfectly. But in our ordinary daily lives, we can see these patterns playing out as well. When we are stuck walking along, being downcast, consumed by our own defeated state, feeling sorry for ourselves, Jesus repeatedly tries to walk with us and ask us what we are talking about to ourselves. If we can start getting in the habit of telling him, the story starts to take a new turn. When, like Thomas, we allow the Lord to show us his own wounds in the people around us who suffer on a daily basis, our attention is shifted away from the reasons we have to be turned in on ourselves and outward toward others, in love. Our own guards are let down and we can begin to say with him, "My Lord and my God!"

In the final chapter of this book, we will consider the part we are to play in the mission and work of the Church in order to bring others into this same healing encounter with the Sacred Heart of Christ.

Mother Teresa Prayer

Dear Jesus, help me to spread Thy fragrance everywhere I go. Flood my soul with Thy spirit and love. Penetrate and possess my whole being so utterly that all my life may only be a radiance of Thine.

Shine through me and be so in me that every soul I come in contact with may feel Thy presence in my soul. Let them look up and see no longer me but only Jesus. Stay with me and then I shall begin to shine as you shine, so to shine as to be a light to others.

Questions and Reflections

1. What are the most powerful and effective words you have ever spoken to another person? How was your heart engaged in those words? What impact did those words have on your concrete life?

2. When have you surrendered yourself to God? To another person? What was it like to experience that fear and great desire? Savor in your memory the sense of freedom that came with that surrender.

3. The next time you go to Mass, see your own heart being placed on that altar along with Jesus' heart. Visualize yourself being given away for others so that they might live. Watch that Communion line. Watch how Jesus is giving away everything he's got for all kinds of people. How can you live like that when you get sent out of the church at the end of Mass with a mission?

Communion and Mission

. . .

When they had finished breakfast, Jesus said to Simon Peter, "Simon, son of John, do you love me more than these?" He said to him, "Yes, Lord, you know that I love you." He said to him, "Feed my lambs."

—John 21:15

Now I rejoice in my sufferings for your sake, and in my flesh I am filling up what is lacking in the afflictions of Christ.

—Colossians 1:24

There is perhaps no greater sign of God's boundless love than the extent to which he was willing to go to save us: becoming small and poor, a baby in the womb of a young, unmarried woman; living in all poverty and humility; abandoned on the Cross; and suffering and dying in disrepute alongside two common criminals.

And yet, even this was not the full story. God's poverty is shown again by his relying on us, the followers of Christ, to have our own sufferings in daily life complete his sufferings. The Father waits, as it were, for us to complete the mission that he gave to his Son to suffer and die, so that the world would be saved. If the world is to be saved, then, we too must suffer. We must offer our own hearts to the world.

This is big. It means our lives mean something. Indeed, our lives mean everything! You and I are necessary for the salvation of the whole world. We are in this together. All those in need around the world need you and me to be united with them, not only by doing good works for them and not only by praying for them, although we must do those things too. But ultimately, people around the world, people we will never meet, depend on us uniting our hearts, especially our suffering, with theirs.

At the same time, people around the world are offering their sufferings in union with you and me when we go through our own difficulties, trials that often seem pointless and make us feel deeply alone and forgotten. No suffering or defeat is forgotten. None of it is pointless. Christ, our head, has united himself to all of us in our defeats. And the Body of Christ, that is, you and me, the whole Church, is also united to these sufferings and defeats.

A couple of things follow from this vision for our daily prayer. First of all, it's good to know that this is the vision! We offer ourselves, particularly our sufferings, in union with Jesus and others who are offering themselves, for the good of others throughout the world, whether inside or outside the Church.

Second, we have to work at reminding ourselves of the vision every day. We have to remember that our daily lives—not just the impressive, successful parts but also the nitty-gritty that includes the confusion and apparent defeats, our prayers and our works, and our joys and our sufferings—are all part of the one mission that the Father gave to the Son and that the Son has given to us: to save the world.

Each one of us is necessary if the mission is to be fulfilled. And it will be fulfilled. It is already fulfilled by Jesus on the Cross, and yet it also needs to be completed in the history. We need to remember this.

This united effort to save the world is why both the Morning Offering and the evening Examen are so essential. This pair of simple prayers during the day renews the vision. We remember what we're a part of and what our lives mean within the life of Christ. This remembering is most perfectly enacted when we go to Mass. All the apparent loose ends of our daily lives are brought together at the altar every time we take part in the Mass.

In the third Eucharistic Prayer, the priest speaks to the Father in the person of the Son, praying not only for ourselves gathered at that Mass but also for "the peace and salvation of all the world." That's what is at stake here—the salvation of all the world. And it is accomplished by the sacrifice of Christ on the Cross, re-presented on the altar at every Mass, and the sacrifices of our daily, apparently insignificant lives.

This is the one story, and each one of us is an essential character in that story, all of us gathered around the person of Christ who is at the center. He is the one sent to bring all humanity back to the Father, and we are necessary participants in his mission. The mission plays out every day in each corner of the world that you and I occupy.

Drawn into Communion

Having highlighted in the last two chapters the elements of offering and sacrifice as essential to this one mystery of the Christian life that finds its fulfillment in the liturgy, let's turn now to focus on what the whole liturgy points to: Communion. First, let's think about what goes into the liturgy itself and learn the pattern for our lives from that.

Having recalled the words of Jesus at the Last Supper and having been reminded that we ourselves are drawn up into this offering of Christ to the Father, the assembly of the faithful is ready to receive the Lord and be drawn into communion with him and with one another—with the whole Church throughout the world as well as with the angels and saints in heaven. It encompasses both the mystical body of Christ (all those in heaven, tying together heaven and earth) and a "horizontal" communion, incorporating everyone gathered in that local church building as well as our brothers and sisters around the world celebrating the same liturgy; we are all made into "one body, one spirit in Christ."

This reality of our communion is recalled when we pray the Our Father together. The Our Father occurs in the liturgy as a bridge between the conclusion of the Eucharistic Prayer and the beginning of the Communion rite. In that moment, we speak out together the reality of who we are as one family: sons and daughters of the Father and brothers and sisters of Jesus, and through him, brothers and sisters to each other. So we *say* what we will soon *do*, or rather what the Father will do for us, through the gift of the body and blood of his Son, his whole self, which will be given to us so that we might live.

After the Our Father, we affirm our unity by offering a sign of peace to each other. This prepares us to be drawn into the peace that only Christ can accomplish for us and through us. After the sign of peace, we begin what is sometimes called the "fraction rite." This is when the priest and the congregation prays the prayer aloud together, "Lamb of God, you take away the sins of the world, have mercy on us . . . grant us peace." Recalling that Jesus is the sacrificial Lamb who takes away the sins of the world, the priest simultaneously breaks the bread.

This is the breaking of the body of Christ, the lamb that is sacrificed before our very eyes. The body of Christ is "fractured" before us. This breaking is essential to the ritual. The priest doesn't do this just because the host is too big. The breaking of the bread reminds us of what is happening. What we are watching is exactly what the disciples from Emmaus saw. When the bread was broken before them, everything came back into focus: the Last Supper and the Cross where his body was offered up and given for all just as he promised the night before. And the memory comes back that Jesus said he would not only be given up for us but also rise and be with us again. All this happens in this one moment of the fraction rite while the "Lamb of God" is prayed together.

"Lord, I Am Not Worthy"

Once that is complete, and after inaudible prayers to Jesus, the priest genuflects before Christ's Body and Blood lying on the altar before him and then he gets up and tells everyone in the congregation, "Behold, the Lamb of God!" And in the showing to the congregation of the Lamb of God, the people in the congregation have a chance to speak to Jesus from their hearts directly to his Heart that is exposed to them: "Lord I am not worthy that you should enter under my roof, but only say the word and my soul shall be healed." These are the words of the military leader who begged Jesus to come to his house to revive his daughter. Though he had great power in the world, he knew the limits of that power and knew full well that the most important thing in his life, the healing of his own daughter, could only be accomplished by Jesus.

And so he spoke from his heart to Jesus. He spoke humbly, knowing his own limitations, and he also spoke confidently, because his focus at that point had been shifted from himself to

Jesus. This is the context for our own repetition of that prayer
in the Mass. We know that there are major parts of our own
lives that we cannot manage. In fact, the more we pay attention
in daily life, the more we realize that we depend on the grace
of God for everything. It's an illusion that we can take care of
everything on our own.

In a real way, that prayer uttered before Communion is not
only about surrender of control, though it is that. It is also, in
an even deeper way perhaps, about healing of our hearts. That
soldier begged the Lord to come under the roof of his house so
that his daughter might be healed. Before Communion in the
Mass, we beg the Lord to come under the roof that houses our
own hearts, the deepest center of our lives, of ourselves.

Through the Morning Offering and the evening Examen,
over time, we come to recognize where we most need the Lord's
help. We come to see where our hearts are wounded, where
things hurt. We came to know better our "core wounds," those
aspects of our own unique histories that have become places of
vulnerability.

Now, when we come to this moment of communion, our
hearts are precisely in the place we need them to be in order to
invite Jesus "under my roof." This is where Jesus wants to go.
We might not feel comfortable inviting him there, but we know
that's where he most needs to go—to heal us. It's a sensitive
spot, but this is what is required. The healing can't come unless
we deliberately open up to that healing, by allowing the life of
Jesus directly into our lives and our hearts and to be specific in
our conversation with him about where we need his help.

Right before the priest receives Communion, he prays, "May
the body of Christ keep me safe for eternal life. May the blood
of Christ keep me safe for eternal life." This is what's at stake

here in the reception of Communion: eternal life. And this life is possible because God has made himself one of us and is doing everything possible to draw us into a personal, intimate relationship with him so that we might live with him forever.

The book of Revelation speaks of Jesus standing at the door of our hearts, waiting for us to open it to him. "Behold, I stand at the door and knock. If anyone hears my voice and opens the door, [then] I will enter his house and dine with him, and he with me" (Rv 3:20). He wants to enter. But he won't force himself in. He waits to be invited. But he is persistent nonetheless in his knocking.

Receiving Jesus in Communion

Going to Communion can become a repetitive action that we do just because it's Sunday morning and it's what we've always done. And that's not bad. As habits go, it's right at the top of the list. But more is possible. Our going to Communion can have an even greater impact in our lives if we dispose ourselves to receive the Lord in greater intimacy and in light of what is going on in our own particular lives at the moment.

A priest often has a particular intention in mind when he celebrates a Mass. Sometimes he knows the person he is praying for—sometimes not. It might be for the repose of somebody's soul. Maybe somebody's mother died and the family asked for a Mass to be said for her. As a relatively young priest, I can tell you that it makes a big difference for me when I'm offering a Mass for a particular person or special intention. When I imagine that particular person's life or health, or whatever the intention is, being offered to the Trinity to be united to Jesus and through

Jesus to be brought to the Father in the unity of the Holy Spirit, the action of the Mass becomes personal and unique.

Elevating our actions at Mass by attaching them to a specific intention isn't just for priests. Every person can speak his or her intention to Jesus at Mass, commending this or that person to the Lord. We can simply hand that person over to the action of the Holy Trinity, drawing all things into God's Self in the liturgy. Let the Father, Son, and Holy Spirit manage that need.

Or maybe your intention is that particular place in your own heart that needs healing. Ask Jesus to come to that little corner of your heart at Communion time. *Come here, Lord, please.* Such prayer is a beautiful, powerful, and simple act on our part. It's a way we can participate in the Mass with great impact for good. When I start coming into the Mass with those particularities in mind and heart, the Mass can't be simply a repetitive action anymore. It is the same liturgy, but it becomes new every time as well.

Receiving What the Lord Wants to Give

When we maintain a daily pattern of morning and evening prayer, we come to know where the Lord wants to go and where we most need him in our own hearts. When we become conscious of these things, the Rite of Communion takes on new meaning. The rubrics of the Mass are not a laundry list of petty rules and unnecessary ways of trying to control us but rather practices with tremendous spiritual significance, developed over the centuries.

Perhaps the most obvious rubric here—one that we don't even think about—is that we have to *receive* Communion. The

Body and Blood of Christ have to be *given* to the faithful. We can't *take* the Lord. We can only receive him.

Sometimes, this is a problem. Deep down, we all want control. We want to grab and cling to things, to people, to ideas, to false identities, and even to wounds. We have a way of fixating on all these things and trying to control them.

Think of the ring in the *Lord of the Rings* story—"my precious," as Gollum so creepily called it. Or think about Adam and Eve, in the first chapter of Genesis, grasping at that forbidden fruit. The whole garden was theirs to enjoy, yet they decided to grab the one thing forbidden to them. This grasping tendency runs deep in our family tree.

Receiving the Lord in Communion is the precise counteraction to the grasping of the Garden of Eden. We stand in line with lots of other people who are just as poor and vulnerable as we are; we are standing in line to receive something for which we are not going to pay. When's the last time you stood in line for something that was free? It's a humbling experience.

When I was a kid (and pretty often still!), my favorite thing to do at Mass was to watch everybody in the Communion line. I'd sit, spellbound, to see whether that old person would make it all the way up that aisle with his walker, hunched over and barely going in a straight line. Offering those gnarled, arthritic hands, opened as much as they could open, the old person would receive the Lord. For many elderly people, this is absolutely the central moment of the entire week. The effort they make is heroic.

Young families are also often heroic and inspiring. I'd think about what it took to get all these little people up, fed, dressed, into the car, and into one pew. I have great admiration for young parents doing this. And many of them, maybe for many years, can't pay that much attention in Mass, for they are thinking about all the things I was just mentioning. They may not be all that well disposed to receive the Lord in Communion. Even though they might not have the concentrated thoughts about it, they are living it out in that very moment. The offering is being made. They're in the midst of it. The Lord knows what's going on here, and the offering of young parents is completing the offering of Jesus for the salvation of the world.

It's the same for those who are walking up that aisle alone. The ache in their hearts feels as if nobody is with them, maybe feels both happy for and resentful of those young families in the pew in front of them—that's the kind of heart to take right to the Lord. The pain that might exist in your own heart can also be part of the salvation of the world—if you unite it to the Heart of Christ in that moment of Communion. You are receiving him who let himself be handed over and left to die alone. And yet that aloneness was not the final reality. Remember the story.

That one story encompasses everyone who is walking up that aisle at Communion time. James Joyce said about Catholics, "Here comes everybody!" Here come the old and young, rich and poor. There are those who are obviously happy, full of life, and embedded in many intimate relationships, and there are also those walking up the aisle who seem defeated and are somewhat vacant in the eyes. There are precious, beautiful, brand-new babies, and there are sullen, spaced-out, ornery seventh graders. There are guys there reluctantly only because their girlfriends or wives insist on it. There are black and white, Hispanic and Asian, and those in their hometown where they were born and those who moved here from the other side of the world. Every kind is coming up that aisle. And we're all in the same boat—with our hands out or even our mouths open, waiting to be fed, to be given what cannot be bought or controlled.

I think it's good to recall how *strange* this is. We come to Mass poor and hungry and needing to be fed. There's nothing we can do to control or get what we want here. We must all wait to receive. This goes even for the lay Communion ministers, the "extraordinary ministers of the Eucharist" as we call them now. They, too, must wait to receive. Even the priest is a part of this same reality (though the priest appears to "take" the consecrated host, he is able to receive from Christ only what Christ freely gives though his priest who is uniquely conformed to him).

The offering of the Eucharist to the people of God is, in fact, the *raison d'être* of the priesthood itself, the whole reason we're here. We offer to God the prayers of the people, and then we offer to the people the Word of God and the Body and Blood, everything the Lord has to give us in the Eucharist. But the only way the priest gets to be in that position is if he first surrenders everything.

At his ordination, each priest gives over all that he has, even lying face down in the middle of the church as a sign of dying to his old self in order to be given a new self, to be conformed to the person of Christ himself. And it is *in persona Christ*, in the person of Christ, based on that prior, sacramental, and real surrender of himself at ordination, that the priest is now able to offer what Jesus offers—himself—at the Eucharist. So this whole economy of surrender of self and reception of what is to be given starts with Christ; it is mediated through the priest and then lived by the rest of the Church.

Think also of those lay Communion ministers. They have to receive before they give Communion to everyone else. They can't give away what they don't have. And they can't have anything until they have first received.

So that's what I mean about the gesture of receiving Communion. But to reach back even before that, we recall again, not what we are doing at Communion time but what the Lord is doing. He is not grasping at anything. He is not clinging to his own power and transcendence that his divinity carries with it. As Philippians put it, Jesus "did not regard equality with God something to be grasped. Rather, he emptied himself" (Phil 2:6–7). So Christ is handing everything over to us, not grasping at anything. In fact, he is very intent on giving us everything he's got. Now, once we see that picture, we can turn to ourselves and ask, what is the best way to receive this?

Accepting the Gift

For many of us, the older we get, the harder it can become to receive gifts. We think they put us in a position of indebtedness. We feel as if we must reciprocate somehow. And maybe we don't want to get tangled up into that dynamic unnecessarily.

And yet, if we have been paying attention on a daily basis, we will know we are in need. We will not hesitate to humble ourselves and receive what the Lord wants to give us. The movements of our hearts remind us, with every Morning Offering and Examen, of our need. Coming forward at Communion, poor, humble, open-hearted, and hungry, will become the most natural thing in the world. In fact, things won't feel right if we miss that weekly or even daily experience of opening up to receive what the Lord has to give.

The Body of Christ is offered; it is never forced on us. Nothing happens until we respond, just as the angel Gabriel proposed

God's plan to Mary at the Annunciation and then waited for her response. God waited for her before initiating the plan to save the world. And God waits for us. Waiting for us to say, "Amen."

When we say it, the Lord becomes very small again, small enough to enter under my roof, to enter into my heart. I believe that. He comes into those corners of my heart where I need him most, especially into the darkness and pain of my history and maybe my present condition as well. I say yes to that. I let him in. Amen. He has knocked on the door, and I have opened and said, "Come in, please."

Taking Up the Mission

And spending a little time in quiet after Communion, God sends us on our mission into our own respective corners of the world. "Go!" Go live like this, like what you've just experienced here in the liturgy. Go offer to the world what you just received here. Go knock on the doors of people's hearts, people who are afraid to let anyone in. Don't force yourselves in, but be there. Be ready. Be ready to listen, to speak, and to be quiet. To be small. Make the proposal. Make an offering of yourself, to the Father, and for the world, just like Jesus. We can do that now, with renewed vigor, thanks to what we have just received.

Ordained priests stand in for Christ in the Mass and offer the sacrifice for the baptized people gathered there. The people, in turn, are to act as priests for the rest of the world when they are sent out of the church building. This is the way the mission of the Church works. Lay people are to live and act as priests for the world beyond the Church. They offer to draw others into relationship with Christ and his Father. They offer the sacrifice of hearts opened up to the world in daily life. The pattern of what happens in the Mass can and must be lived out in daily life.

An Invitation

What would it look like in your corner of the world, in your family, at work, at school, and in the clubs or organizations you might belong to, if you would act like a priest and receive the humble gifts brought forward by God's people?

What would it look like if you were then to turn to the Father to thank him for those gifts, to call down the Holy Spirit upon them, and to gradually let Jesus take over?

In other words, what if you took those gifts that you have received in daily life and offered them generously as gifts of love back to the world, to those who most need that love, and to those who are most hungry for it?

Take this and eat it. This is my body.

What I have to give is not from me. It's from the Lord. And what he has given, I freely give over to you. What if this became the way we started to see reality? What if this could slowly start to become our vision for our daily lives, following this pattern of receiving gifts and letting them be transformed, broken open, and then given away?

Life might start to look a lot more interesting, challenging, difficult, and totally worth it. Living like this requires a new kind of heart. And this is exactly what Jesus wants to give us, if we are willing to receive it. All we have to do, in every moment of each day, is to say, "Amen!"

Prayer for Generosity
St. Ignatius of Loyola

> Lord Jesus, teach me to be generous;
> teach me to serve you as you deserve,
> to give and not to count the cost,
> to fight and not to heed the wounds,
> to toil and not to seek for rest,
> to labor and not to seek reward,
> except that of knowing that I do your will.
> Amen.

Questions and Reflections

1. How is some of your most "effective" work in life accomplished only in the surrender of your heart in love? What impact do you have on others, not by what you *do* but by *how* you are with them?

2. What difficult situation are you facing now in your life that you can't make any better by your efforts? Can you surrender to Jesus and just let him work through you?

3. How do you need to *get out of the way* of what Jesus is trying to accomplish through you? Whom does he want to love through you? Whom does he want to reconcile to himself through you? Are you willing to cooperate? Say yes.

The Three Moments:
A Concise Guide

· · ·

Morning Offering

Before getting out of bed, pray a Morning Offering such as this one:

Jesus,

I offer you my day and all that is in it—all the prayers, works, joys, and sufferings I might experience today—in union with your own Heart that is loved by the Father and opened up to the world, even if it gets pierced. I offer you every moment of the day in union also with the intentions of the Holy Father, all the bishops around the world, and all other apostles of prayer, as well as with all those who are suffering today, for the salvation of the world. Amen.

Examen

At the end of the day, review your day with God. Quiet yourself and rest in God's presence a few moments.

- Thank God for a few concrete gifts of the day. Ask for light from the Holy Spirit to remember the day well.

- Review the events of your day, from morning until now, even if for just a few moments. Pay attention to the movements of your heart. Notice where you are surprised and especially grateful for an encounter or experience and where you are ashamed of how you acted in a particular circumstance.

- Thank God again for the good memories. Ask for forgiveness for the bad ones.

- Rest in God's presence a few moments more. Ask for the grace of a peaceful sleep and for the gift of being open-hearted again when you wake up.

Live the Eucharist

If possible, go to Mass today.

Pay close attention to the prayers spoken and movements made, especially of the offertory, when the bread and wine are carried up the aisle from the people in the congregation.

Listen carefully to the consecration, when the priest speaks the word of Jesus: "This is my body . . . this is my blood."

During the fraction rite, where the bread is broken in order to be given away, and Communion itself, when the people come forward to receive Jesus, contemplate the wonder of this mystery: once again, Jesus comes among us to give us his very Self.

Meditate on how you can live your day more deliberately according to this pattern.

How can you let your own heart, united with the Sacred Heart of Jesus, be blessed, broken, and given away freely in daily life? Ask for that grace.

Notes

• • •

1. U2, "When I Look at the World" from *All That You Can't Leave Behind* (Interscope Records, October 2000). Lyrics by Bono and The Edge.

2. Christopher Collins, S.J., "Pedro Arrupe and the Spiritual Renewal of the Society of Jesus: Thirty Years Later," *Review for Religious*, 70.3, 2011.

3. *Gaudium et spes*, 22.

4. Irenaeus of Lyons, *Against Heresies*, III.19.1.

5. Ibid.

6. A list of the pope's intentions for each month may be found on the main menu of the Apostleship of Prayer website, at http://www.apostleshipofprayer.org/.

7. Benedict XVI, General Audience, Paul VI Hall, February 1, 2012.

Christopher Collins, S.J., is the current chair of the board of the Apostleship of Prayer in the United States. A popular speaker, retreat guide, and spiritual director, Collins has traveled all over the country and around the world to promote the devotion to the Sacred Heart and eucharistic spirituality. He entered the Society of Jesus in 1995 and was ordained a priest in 2006. Collins teaches theology and is director of the Catholic studies program at Saint Louis University. *Collins is also the author of The Word Made Love: The Dialogical Theology of Joseph Ratzinger/ Benedict XVI.*

Founded in 1865, Ave Maria Press,
a ministry of the Congregation of
Holy Cross, is a Catholic publishing
company that serves the spiritual and
formative needs of the Church and its
schools, institutions, and ministers;
Christian individuals and families; and
others seeking spiritual nourishment.

———◦———

For a complete listing of titles from

Ave Maria Press

Sorin Books

Forest of Peace

Christian Classics

visit www.avemariapress.com

ave maria press® / Notre Dame, IN 46556
A Ministry of the United States Province of Holy Cross